Praise for
LIFE INSIDE MY MIND

★"Who better to raise teens' awareness of mental illness and health than the YA authors they admire? Their compelling stories will start important discussions and assure readers they're never alone." —*Booklist*, starred review

★"In this much-needed, enlightening book, 31 young adult authors write candidly about mental health crises, either their own or that of someone very close to them. Ranging from humorous to heartbreaking to hopeful, each story has a uniquely individual approach to the set of circumstances that the writer is dealing with." —*School Library Journal*, starred review

★"These bold, brave essays will educate the uninformed and inspire hope in those who may feel alone in their suffering." —*Publisher's Weekly*, starred review

"Teens may be unlikely to seek out this collection on their own, but it is a valuable read to put in the hands of those who need it." —*Kirkus*

"Jessica Burkhart's *Life Inside My Mind* provides a significantly real and much needed discourse on the widespread yet still stigmatized experience of mental illness in its many varied and common forms in our society. The personal words and glimpses into the lives of our most popular YA authors will hopefully serve to both educate and normalize the reality of these common emotional conditions and bring some peace, hope, and lovingkindness to all those who read them." —Lisa Schab, author of *The Self Esteem Habit for Teens*

"This book emphasizes that many people live with mental health issues and that, despite the ignorance about and negativity toward mental illness, there is nothing of which they should be ashamed. Writers of these essays offer support by demonstrating that they are survivors who are willing to acknowledge and discuss their different illnesses. These are important messages to make available to teens."   —*VOYA*

"For teens who are suffering, though, these authors prove that, with the help of friends, professionals, and/or the right combination of meds, people with mental health issues can flourish, attain success, and help others by sharing their stories, whether personal or creative."   —*BCCB*

LIFE INSIDE MY MIND

31 AUTHORS SHARE THEIR PERSONAL STRUGGLES

edited by Jessica Burkhart

Simon Pulse

New York   London   Toronto   Sydney   New Delhi

SIMON PULSE

An imprint of Simon & Schuster Children's Publishing Division

1230 Avenue of the Americas, New York, New York 10020

First Simon Pulse paperback edition April 2019

For information about special discounts for bulk purchases, please contact Simon & Schuster Special Sales at 1-866-506-1949 or business@simonandschuster.com.

The Simon & Schuster Speakers Bureau can bring authors to your live event. For more information or to book an event, contact the Simon & Schuster Speakers Bureau at 1-866-248-3049 or visit our website at www.simonspeakers.com.

Book designed by Steve Scott

The text of this book was set in Hiroshige.

Manufactured in the United States of America

2 4 6 8 10 9 7 5 3 1

Library of Congress Control Number 2018930091

ISBN 978-1-4814-9464-9 (hc)

ISBN 978-1-4814-9465-6 (pbk)

ISBN 978-1-4814-9466-3 (eBook)

APR 2 3 2019

This collection is dedicated to any readers who

have ever dealt with any form of mental illness.

May you find comfort and strength through

the experiences shared in these pages.

Contents

CONTENTS

LIFE
INSIDE
MY
MIND

Stupid Monsters and Child Surgeons

by
Maureen
Johnson

I have had anxiety. I suffered a serious bout of it a few years ago. It hit me like a bolt out of the blue and stuck with me for a while.

If you have anxiety, you may know that reading about anxiety usually makes more anxiety. When I had anxiety, I could not read about anxiety without getting anxiety, and yet I read about it pretty compulsively, looking for answers. I was looking for something that told me there was a light at the end of the tunnel. I am letting you know that this essay has that light. It has a sunrise. I know that matters. Trust me. Hold my hand as we go, if you want to go with me.

Anxiety bouts can end. They end all the time. Never give up hope that yours can and will end. I am not a mental health professional, and if you are suffering from severe anxiety, I strongly, strongly suggest seeing one. You may already be doing so. Also, what I write about here is what happened to me. We are all different, and your mileage may vary. Anxiety has a lot of causes and pathways. There is no one way to deal with it—which is good. There are a LOT of ways. Millions—billions?—of people deal with anxiety. Almost all of us deal with some form of mental infirmity at one point or another in our lives. You're not only not alone—you're in the majority.

I want you to know that people can have it and do lots of stuff and actually be happy. I want you to know that exists.

I want you to know it is not all bad. I swear I am not making this up. I want you to know the bout of anxiety that I thought would crush me may have been one of the very best things that ever happened to me. It can be useful.

Now I'll just tell you my story, and if it is of use to you, that's good.

So what happened was that things were going pretty well for me when the anxiety hit. Before then, I thought I knew what anxiety was. I thought it was that feeling I'd had before tests, or in certain situations. I thought it was just that nervous feeling. I soon learned that anxiety was a very weird beast.

It came on first as some strange sensations—pounding in the chest, things that felt like electrical shocks going down my arms. At the time, I was working a lot. I thought nothing of sitting at my desk until midnight or later, pounding away. My brain was going and going like a train, and then these shocks would come on. It really felt like I had been hit with a bolt of juice right out of a power outlet. Then came the panic attacks in the night, when I would wake up with my heart racing, feeling like I couldn't breathe. They got more and more frequent. Then I was often up at five a.m., pacing around. And then one day I had one of those that didn't shut off when I woke up. My body was racing. What was most disturbing was that suddenly I didn't feel like I was in control of my thoughts. It was like I had always been in the driver's seat of my brain, and then one morning it was hijacked. I was shoved to the passenger's seat. I could see where we were going, but I couldn't steer. Almost as if I was watching myself think. I was filled with dread and energy, and I had no idea why. My brain was veering around all over the place.

This all happened on a beautiful summer's day. I was supposed to meet two friends to write. I got myself dressed and went out. I called my mother (who is a nurse) and spoke to her. I was teary and shaking. I tried to work, but the words were moving around on the page in front of me. I told my friends what was going on, and they were very helpful. I felt like I had to walk. They walked with me for a few hours, and then one of them got in a cab with me and took me to the doctor. (The doctor had already checked me over for the symptoms I'd been having. He had concluded I had anxiety.)

I was given Ativan that night. My mother came up to stay with me—I was in that much of a state of distress. I took the pill. My system slowed down a bit for the night and kicked up again the next day. This was the start of months of this. I won't go through the bad stuff and all the thoughts I had, because you probably already know them if you have been through it.

3

I did wonder a lot about how I was going to do anything, how I was going to live my life and do my job. I wondered how I was going to go to bed, and then what would happen when I woke up. These are the kinds of fun times anxiety gives you. It's a jerk. During that summer, writing was hard. I couldn't focus very well. Then I got angry, and I attacked the anxiety. I attacked it with EVERYTHING I COULD FIND. I said, "I have decided this anxiety is a signal that I need to do something, so I am going to do it."

Let me tell you what I learned and WHAT I DID ABOUT IT, because that is what matters.

First, the anxiety is not you. It's drifting around you, but it's not you. I like to imagine anxiety as the big red monster from Bugs Bunny. (Google this if you want the visual.) It sits outside you. It's kind of ridiculous-looking. The anxiety may be with you now, but it can just as easily go away. It is not a permanent part of you, no matter how it seems.

Second thing: You know how depression lies? Well, anxiety is stupid. I did not just say people with anxiety are stupid. No, no. I mean that anxiety *itself* is stupid. If you asked anxiety what two plus two is, anxiety will think very hard and then say "triangle" or "a bag of Fritos" or "a commemorative stamp." Because anxiety doesn't know what anything is. It will try to convince you that things that are totally fine are worthy of dread. That summer, when it was bad, it didn't matter what I looked at or engaged in at first; the anxiety monster was scared of it. It was scared of busy situations, accidents, spiders, sleeping, being awake, my sneakers, the wall . . . I caught on to the stupidity thing the day I broke down and watched the most boring nature show I could possibly find, just to slow my mind down. It was just pretty pictures of mountains and trees. An anxiety attack came on as I was watching, and I said to it, "You are totally stupid. Nothing this stupid can defeat me. You're going down, you idiotic monster. I AM RULER HERE!"

Another helpful visual: I started to think of anxiety as being very, very small, like a child in an oversize lab coat who was trying to order me around. "You're adorable, kid," I said. "Now let's go find your parents. Or maybe put you in an orphanage."[1]

With that realization, anxiety was genuinely put on notice.

Third: I looked around at my life and situation. I saw a few things clearly for the first time. For a start, I had no boundaries between work and life. I had no time limits. I would stay online until all hours and let my brain drink in the electricity. There is a lot of research (so much I can't just link here) that indicates this is not super good for our brains. I started to set limits. I stopped work at certain hours, no matter what. If the anxiety had made it hard to write during the day, I didn't try again at night. I stopped.

I slowed down everything. I put myself on a gentler mental

---

[1] I do not condone putting misbehaving children into orphanages, unless they are imaginary misbehaving children who live in your head. And my imaginary orphanage for imaginary children is a very nice place.

diet, and I didn't care who knew it. If it was slow and boring and something that would be enjoyed in a nursing home, then it was for me. I adopted what I called the Grandma Lifestyle, and I've never looked back. This idea that we have to be Doing! Things! All! The! Time! is bullshit. That's television talking to you, or articles, or the persistent but false impression that literally everyone is out accomplishing more and doing more and loving it all 100 PERCENT OF THE TIME!!! Lies. People do some things using various units of time and under all kinds of conditions. This is not a competition, and there is no metric.

I walked slowly. I went out and looked at whatever there was to see. A tree. A duck. Storefronts. Other people. I dialed it all back and stopped judging what I had to be reading/doing/thinking/appreciating and suddenly realized I had a lot of weird ideas about what I "had" to do. I'd been knocking myself around and making myself jump through hoops to accomplish things that had no discernible benefit. I didn't learn this in one day. It took a few months. My thoughts began to clear, and I was able to do more and more. And a major part of the way I got there was through meditation.

That's four: meditation. And it is a BIG ONE. I know. It's in magazines at Whole Foods and it's everywhere and trendy, but you know what? It changed my life, and I do it every day. Again, plenty of science out there you can easily find online. You need to be consistent. This is the key. You don't just do it once and then you're changed. It is like exercise. I tell you true I know it changed my way of thinking and has probably physically changed my brain. It is part of my life to this day and will remain so.[2]

Five: I got help. I went to the doctor and got medication that I was on for about a year and a half, and I did cognitive behavioral therapy, which helped me break down my thought patterns. I also had a more serious look at WHY I was so burned-out and exhausted and found the medical problem that was really at the root of all of this. Which was a good thing. I mean, it's annoying, but it's good to know, because I can do something about it.

Six: I exercised. I started going to yoga classes a lot. Which, again, seems like a cliché but does in fact work. I walked. I just moved. I also cut back on caffeine a tremendous amount. I had been drinking QUITE A LOT OF COFFEE up until that point. (I probably could do five to eight cups a day.) I stopped entirely for about two years. Now I drink a limited amount and never in the evening. So yes, sensible diet and sensible steps that are all boring but REALLY WORK. But they work over time.

Seven: KNOW THAT IT CAN END. It will tell you that it won't. Remember: IT DOESN'T KNOW ANYTHING. Anxiety is like a four-year-old who thinks they are a surgeon—

---

[2] I have taken several types of meditation classes or programs in the last few years. I really went for it. The ones I recommend most are mindfulness-based stress reduction (often labeled as MBSR) classes. There are also free or quite cheap apps available, and loads of places offer free or very cheap classes. Have a look around your area. Many libraries will have books on meditation as well. There is no bad way to get started, and it is often worth trying a few things to see what works for you.

that's cute that the child thinks that, but you wouldn't actually let the four-year-old operate on you. THE CHILD KNOWS NOTHING. You would prevent the child from attempting any surgical procedure. Likewise, anxiety must be prevented from making your decisions. It's so small! It's so silly! Look how it thinks it can move you around! You can regain control. It really isn't stronger than you.

Eight: I found out just how many other people had it. Seeing it was not just me really was a great eye-opener. Someone around you has anxiety right now as well. You may or may not know about it. People doing all kinds of things have anxiety. Some of the people who make the shows you like have or had it. Same with the people who write the songs you like or the books you like. People doing all kinds of jobs have or had it. It is super common. It moves around. It can be lived with and shown the door. You are not alone in this.

Nine: There is nothing to be embarrassed about. So what if you are hiding in a bathroom stall because you've panicked about seeing a menu? SO WHAT. So what if you are talking fast? SO WHAT. So what if you wrote a long and nervous-sounding post? SO WHAT. So what if you couldn't finish something because you had an anxiety attack while looking at a pen? SO WHAT. Doesn't matter. I've been there. Come on out when you're ready, and we'll throw that pen out the window. Or we'll say, "It's okay—you're a nice pen." SO WHAT. Say SO WHAT right now. Because SO WHAT. Unless you just caused a major international incident, which I promise you you did not (unless you are Vladimir Putin reading this, in which case I have severely misjudged my audience), you didn't do anything awful and no one cares and SO WHAT!

I had to throw a whole bunch of stuff at it. Together, it worked. The severe, continuous bouts stopped after a few months. I remained on alert for at least a year or two, but I genuinely cannot remember if I had attacks during that time. Because part of what happened was that I stopped being afraid of it. I gave it permission to come and go. I left the door open. "You can come in," I said, "and you can show yourself out." Sounds stupid and New Agey, but it is a TRUE STATEMENT. I just decided I didn't care anymore and was going to go about my business whether it was there or not. It took effort, but I stuck with that. And the monster wandered off on its stupid way.

But I don't hate it. Remember I said there was good stuff? There was.

I'm frankly a better person for having had it. I'm not saying I am a fantastic person—that is not for me to decide. But I felt the sting, and I got a lot more compassionate. I realized that since I had this major disruption, I might as well use the time to make some changes. It's like, *Well, the roof of my house just came off. I guess I'll redecorate!* This is possible. You can make it do something for you, since it is there. Give that stupid monster a broom and MAKE IT CLEAN. I slowed the hell down, and I like stuff more now. I give no f**ks about what people think of my slow-life choices.

When I did this, I looked around at what I had and saw that life is pretty great and things can change. I thought I couldn't do anything when I had it, and I look back and see that I did lots of things. Was I slower? Yes. But do I still get my stuff done? Yes. I work more efficiently now.

I realized that when I wasn't staring at the anxiety all the time, I was happy. I had convinced myself for a while that it was not possible to be both, but that's a lie. You may think that is true because the anxiety is dancing around like a big dumb idiot, trying to block your view of happy. But happy can be there. It probably is there. CONTENT is there. NON-ANXIETY is definitely there.

Again, this is my story, and all the stories are different. But like I said, I tell this one to give you a true story about having anxiety that ends with something good, which happens to be true. A lot of you are going to deal with it, and you can make that stupid monster dance. You can make good changes. Or you can just be okay. You can. Don't listen to it when it tells you you can't, because remember: It is stupid and you are not. It doesn't know a thing. It really doesn't. Whatever happens, SO WHAT.

Good luck out there, and give no f**ks you do not want to give.

Twenty Pills

by Robison Wells

I take twenty pills a day, and each one tells a story.

I know there will be readers who will criticize my decision to use so many drugs. They will tell me that I ought to use some other treatment regimen—that I'm becoming an over-medicated zombie.

I'm not against other treatments: I am a believer in cognitive behavioral therapy; I have a psychiatric service dog; I meditate. But I also take medicine, and I don't apologize for it. I find that most of the people who criticize meds also try to sell me essential oils and egg powder, or they tell me to think happier thoughts. Yes, I don't like the side effects of the meds—three of my prescriptions are taken solely to treat the side effects of the other meds—but, in my experience, taking meds helps more than not.

Not all of my drugs have been good. As anyone who's ever had to take psychoactive meds can tell you, it's not an exact science. I went through four different antidepressants before I found one that worked. You try one for two or three months to see if it helps, and when it doesn't, you try something else.

So that's the first one I'm going to talk about: my antidepressants. I take escitalopram, two pills a night. I'm not terribly depressed—it comes and goes—but an antidepressant is kind of the foundation of every mental illness treatment. It balances the chemicals in your brain that are out of balance. (I'm not a doctor. I don't understand exactly what chemical does what. But that's what I've gathered in the past six and a half years that I've been sick.)

I'm only mildly acquainted with depression. I work from home as a full-time writer. Depression usually makes me park myself on the couch and watch TV, or traps me at my desk when I'm trying to work. I do a lot of staring. A lot of time-wasting activities that help me mute out the world. I spend inordinate amounts of time on Facebook or Twitter or Wikipedia. I feel sad. I feel that I'm a failure. I feel that my books are terrible. I feel like I'll never get better. I feel that the world would be better without me in it. Fortunately, those latter feelings are relatively rare. I've never tried to kill myself.

I did admit myself into a psych ward once, because I was so sick that I didn't know what else I could possibly do. It was an odd experience. The rooms are designed to make it impossible to kill yourself. They take away everything you have, give you a strip search, making certain that you don't have anything that could be a weapon or a noose. The doors are sloped, so if you were to have a rope, and you wanted to hang yourself, you and your rope would slide off the door. I also noticed that the electrical outlets and light switches were nailed into the wall, not screwed. Sharp corners were padded. The toilet was just behind a partition so that you couldn't hide in a bathroom and do harmful things.

I got out of there as quickly as I could. And my antidepressant does its job most of the time.

One side effect of my antidepressant is weight gain: I've gained eighty pounds in the six years that I've been sick. So I take phentermine (one pill thirty minutes before breakfast.) It's a stimulant that reduces my appetite. It works. I rarely remember to eat lunch, and sometimes breakfast. Around dinnertime I recognize that I'm shaking and sick, and my wife tells me my blood sugar is low, and I go eat something. (Not a perfect diet plan, but it seems to be working.)

I had been on Topamax, a drug that makes you lose tons of weight, but it also can make you dumb. It's jokingly referred to as the "skinny and stupid" drug. Unlike phentermine, where doctors can explain how a stimulant suppresses your appetite, nobody's really sure how Topamax works. That's a common thread that runs throughout all of these meds. Nobody knows what will work and what won't. You're treated through trial and error. I was on Topamax for a year (three pills a day), and in that year the police gave me three tickets, not including the morning I got pulled over for a possible DUI. I had to do all of those sobriety tests that you see on TV. (I swear I don't know how anyone is expected to recite the alphabet backward, sober or not.) Fortunately, I passed well enough to not get arrested. But I did get into three car accidents that year, which led to a loss of my driver's license.

Even though I had lost thirty pounds, I asked my doctor to take me off Topamax—I simply couldn't write. That entire year is a cloudy mess that I can barely remember. I traveled to Paris for a book festival—my only time ever in Europe—and I remember virtually nothing from my time there. I know I fell asleep in Notre Dame (and they kicked me out), then I went across the street to a café, where I fell asleep again (and they kicked me out). That was typical of my experience with Topamax. On the flight home I took my handful of pills and was so motionless that the woman next to me thought I had tried to kill myself, and they made one of those "Is there a doctor on the plane?" announcements. I woke at the end of the flight with a nurse monitoring me.

Going all the way back to the beginning, in 2010, my problems first manifested with a severe panic disorder and agoraphobia. Panic disorder is all anxiety, all the time. Your fight-or-flight response is always switched on. Panic attacks feel a lot like heart attacks—chest pain, hyperventilating, sweating, dizziness, et cetera—only with the added feature of intense fear. Agoraphobia is the fear of situations where a panic attack might occur—crowds, stressful situations, social settings. Anything, really. I have a terrible time with church: I generally only last twenty or thirty minutes before I have to get up and leave. I once got trapped in a Home Depot, where I had the few things I needed to buy but couldn't bring myself to go up to the front of the store—either to go to the checkout counter or just leave. I ended up sitting in the back, on the floor next to the insulation, crying for an hour. It got so bad that I couldn't go into conference rooms at work. I would sit on the floor of my cubicle. I lost my job. In retrospect, I probably could have sued for getting fired because I was disabled, but I didn't.

That led to Klonopin, one of the benzodiazepines (often called "benzos"). Others I tried: alprazolam, diazepam, lorazepam. They all do the same thing (in different enough ways that some work and some don't), which is stop a panic attack. I take three pills every night if it's been a good day, but if I get an attack, I'll take an additional five to try to squash it. A friend, Howard Tayler, calls me a Klonopiñata: If you hit me, Klonopin falls out. My doctor doesn't like that I take so much, and we both recognize that I'm developing a tolerance to it (obviously—no one ought to take eight Klonopin a day). So I'm supposed to cut back, which I totally would do if I stopped getting panic attacks four times a week.

The big drug I'm on now is ziprasidone, an antipsychotic (two capsules every night). It's for obsessive-compulsive disorder, which is not anything like you've probably seen it described. (Usually, people say "I'm a little OCD" when what they mean is that they like things tidy.) The obsessive part of OCD is when a person has intrusive thoughts that hinder their ability to function normally. The compulsion part is when you must perform some sort of ritualistic behavior to, inexplicably, free you from the obsession. I've had lots of constant, intrusive thoughts. I used to stare out my back window and watch the mountain explode and collapse like Mount Saint Helens. I used to keep an eye on my car's rearview mirror because I knew someone was following me. When I'm home all alone, I have auditory hallucinations: I hear the Dave Matthews Band's "Typical Situation" playing; my service dog talks to me. There was a time when I couldn't ever sit still, and I'd work fourteen hours a day, only coming home from the office to sleep. And the compulsions! They deserve their own paragraph.

I remember one evening sitting on the couch with my wife when she mused, "You know what I'd really like right now? A caramel Oreo shake." And I remember thinking, *You know what I'd really like right now? To punch myself in the face.* That action—specifically, bleeding from my head—sounded as good to me as ice cream. I knew that if I just punched myself in the face, maybe breaking the skin above my eye or bloodying my nose, everything would be so much better. I felt like I had pressure building up inside me, and the only way to release it was to bleed it out.

Once that was mostly under control, self-harm reared its ugly head back up with dermatillomania, a compulsion to dig into my scalp with my fingernails and bleed. And not just in the back, under the hair, but front and center, at the top of the forehead. So when I showed up at my psychiatrist's office with a big, bloody scar on my head, he put me on another antipsychotic, used to treat delusions (two pills: one in the morning, one at night). It's a strong drug, with troubling potential side effects—I asked the doctor what I should look for, and he told me that by the time I realized something was wrong, I could be unconscious with my heart stopped.

Which brings me to the final drugs: propranolol (three tablets at bedtime) and benztropine (two tablets at bedtime). Both treat side effects. The first reduces a need to pace and walk around, and the second gets rid of needlelike sensations similar to restless legs syndrome.

And if I did my math right, that's twenty pills. There's one last side effect: sleepwalking. My doctor's only guess about that one is that it's caused not by any particular med but by the sheer volume of pills I take before bed every night.

Some of my conditions have a good prognosis: Panic disorder can be cured completely. My dermatillomania is all but gone. However, there's no cure for OCD. Odds are I'll be living with that one for the rest of my life. On the other hand, researchers say our understanding of the brain is fifty years behind our understanding of any other organ. Who's to say some new drug might not be on the market in the near future?

I'll be first in line.

Light and Dark

by
Lauren
Oliver

I don't remember the first time I was depressed, really depressed, although I know it must have been in middle school. I do remember a day in eighth grade, heading with my mom beneath a violently colorful spring sky, when I scanned the clouds for signs about whether I should kill myself.

My adolescence and early adulthood were filled with fantasies of death. Smashed beneath the wheels of a car, falling from a high ledge, shot by a random stranger: In many of my fantasies I was a passive player, the victim of circumstances beyond my control. Over time my fantasies grew more specific and also more resonant—I imagined overdosing or cutting my wrists to bleed out in a bathtub, a dangerous form of mental playacting for a girl who by then was cutting her wrists often, sometimes without looking to see what I would hit.

I don't remember when it started; it was a song I heard that, like an earworm, just buried itself into who I was, into my consciousness. There were temporary reprieves, bursts of happiness and triumph, but these were more like the delirium that certain fever patients experience as their illness progresses: The sickness had infected even the way I learned to be happy, by escape, by deadening coupling with anonymous partners, by recklessness and a kind of furious ecstasy.

In the same way that I don't remember when it started, I don't remember when it began to get better, although it wasn't without effort. I still take medication. Although I no longer go to therapy, I did for the better part of two decades and would certainly return immediately if I needed it.

I do remember another spring day, nearly twenty years after the day I had looked up into the clouds for a sign of whether to die, when, on a run in Prospect Park, I suddenly stopped with a short gasp of surprise and noted nothing but a hollow echo in my head, like the sound of the wind running through an empty shell.

The song, the miserable song that told me I was unloved and unlovable, that I was alone, that my life would feel like one long desert slowly scorching my ability to scream, was gone. It had just . . . vanished. Poof. I finished my run in a sense of wonder, but also confusion. How had I lived with that horrible wailing for so long? Was this, lightness and freedom, what other people felt all the time?

Mental illness—having it, advocating for its understanding, living with it—has an image problem. A large part of the problem, I think, is the term itself—illness is something that automatically suggests rot and contagion, a short interim of bodily collapse that must and can be cured as quickly as possible. But the spectrum of mental disorders—which runs from low-grade depression to personality disorders to acute schizophrenia—suggests that this term is far from sufficient.

It is far too restrictive. It suggests two states, and only two states: healthy and sick, well and unwell.

But the truth is many people who live with mental illness are well *and* sick. I will always be prone to depression and treat it like a chronic illness by addressing it with medication; I am also well in any coherent sense of the word. And I think that's why, when sitting down to write this essay, I felt initially a kind of resistance, a stubborn desire to say nothing, or that I had nothing to say.

There was a time when I was ashamed of my depression and hid it. Then there was a time I celebrated it and believed it defined me. Now I feel it is nothing to be ashamed of and also nothing that defines me. In fact, it has nothing to do with who I am at all. I am not responsible for an annoying song that gets stuck in my head, though I may take steps to try to forget it. But the song has no meaning to me. It doesn't make me who I am. It's just mental process and how our brains cycle through information. Certain things get stuck, sometimes for long periods of time. Better, perhaps, to term mental illness "mental *stutters*"—it is both less accusatory and less comprehensively descriptive. If you are mentally ill, then there is something wrong with you. If you have mental stutters, well . . . who doesn't trip up sometimes?

This, I think, would help resolve one of the biggest crises that advocacy for mental health faces: the idea that mentally ill people can be defined as one thing and can be, more importantly, *understood totally through the lens of their illness.* People who suffer from mental illness of all varieties are still people. Their mental stutters may be bigger or smaller. They may occasionally be so large that they trip people into modes of behavior that are obsessive or even frightening. But people cannot be understood through the lens of mental illness any more than they can be understood through the lens of their colds, or their cancers.

On the other hand, people can be understood through— and tend to react similarly to—shame, alienation, and a sense of being profoundly alone. It's entirely possible that when people with mental illness—or stutters—do commit violence, against themselves or others, they are reacting as much to the societal rebuffing they have experienced as they are to the song that is stuck replaying in their heads.

I have some mental stutters. Who doesn't? We are all living with a unique constellation of strengths and defects. It is nothing to be ashamed or proud of; it is a natural phenomenon, like the real constellations that obey their own laws and bring light and strangeness to an otherwise dark universe.

Escape Clause

by Jennifer L. Armentrout

There are days when I'm not very active on social media, but I'm normally there, just being the best Twitter creeper I can be. This one night was different, though, and has stood out months later. Twitterworld was blowing up about a book description that was just released, and while many, many people were making very valid points about certain words and phrases used, the conversation turned to how one of the characters described himself as being broken. Now, if I remember correctly, the character wasn't dealing with mental illness, but somehow the conversation turned to depression. Some in the bookish community, mainly other authors, were speaking out about how offensive and wrong it was to use the word "broken" when describing how a character/person felt about their mental health issues.

I remember feeling this shivery sensation crawling up my spine and spreading over the base of my skull as I read tweet

22

after tweet from people stating how wrong it was to feel and/or say that. This, of course, wasn't the first time Twitterworld got so wrapped up in policing feelings/thoughts on everything that the entire conversation went off the rails and entered straight into Not-Touching-That-With-a-Ten-Foot-Pole Land, ticket for one, but it was another example of how we get so caught up in wanting our own stories and experiences *heard* that we fail to *listen*, to empathize. We're so set on being right we don't necessarily realize we're failing to remember that not all experiences are the same, especially, *especially* when it comes to mental health issues. We fail to realize that sometimes we're "othering" people when actually discussing "othering" of people.

We also forget, even as authors, the power and perception of words.

There was something incredibly triggering about reading those tweets from people who genuinely mean well, but who may be doing more harm than good in the way they discuss mental health issues. And in my case and many others, it was doing a whole hell of a lot of harm.

All I could think was what would the seventeen-year-old Jen think and feel seeing tweets from people she admired saying that how she felt about herself was not only wrong but offensive? Then I thought about all the other people out there who have felt broken or wired wrong, who didn't feel normal or even *right*, and what a kick in the stomach that would be to now see people saying that their feelings were an insult to others.

As if anyone needs yet another reason to feel bad about themselves.

Feeling broken or as if something is wrong with you doesn't necessarily equate to feeling less than someone else. Nor does feeling this way now mean you'll always feel this way. But it never, NEVER means how you feel about your own experiences with depression or any mental health issue is offensive or insulting to others. Because it's not about them. It's about you. They can exit stage left stat.

Most people who are familiar with mental health issues know you have to be so careful when talking about these things, so damn careful. Any psychologist, friend, or human being who's done the basic research into mental illness knows that no part of treatment involves telling someone they're offensive or insulting. It's remapping the way you feel about yourself and developing better coping mechanisms. It's about correcting these core beliefs.

I wanted to start carpet-bombing Twitter. Well, I sort of did. Not just because I studied psychology or worked in the mental health field, but because I know what it's like to experience depression in silence. To bottle up all those dark thoughts and experiences, sit back and watch everyone else talk about it while not being comfortable enough to come forward and share my own experiences with depression. I know what it's like to have an Escape Clause.

Not the cool one in the Santa Clause movies.

The Escape Clause is a plan—a plan B, so to speak—that

has lingered in the recesses of my mind since I was a teenager, surfacing whenever my life feels like a washing machine on an erratic, never-ending spin cycle.

"Escape Clause" is just a code, a way to make me feel better about what those two words really mean. It's like taking something ugly and terrifying, and prettying it up. Hanging a paper lantern on it. Those two words cover up the fact that I still break out in cold sweats whenever I think about what it truly stands for and what I can be capable of in the darkest moments.

The Escape Clause is me deciding to get off this ride, to check out when I feel like I just don't want to do this anymore, any of this. It's the next step that pops into my head when something fails or there's bad news or I'm too stressed out or . . . well, I could keep going. It's always there. Sometimes it's like an annoying gnat you can just bitch-slap into next year. Other times, it's the size of an elephant stomping its feet and can't be ignored.

While anxiety is like a faulty house alarm that keeps going off even though no one is breaking into the house, for me, depression is like that stage-five-clinger, toxic friend who comes around every so often and is super hard to shake. It's always there, waiting for that perfect moment to pop back into my life. It revels in misery and negativity, and the Escape Clause is a master of lies. It tells me no one cares, nothing matters, I'll never be good enough, the responsibilities and deadlines are all too much, and everything would be better if it were all over. There're four things you need to know about the Escape Clause and me.

1. The Escape Clause is literally the shittiest coping mechanism known to man.
2. The Escape Clause is depression.
3. The Escape Clause is suicide.
4. The Escape Clause is well hidden in me, because it represents a part of me that very few people are aware of.

You see, people don't think of suicide and depression when they think of me. Other than my chronic resting bitch face on panels, I'm always smiling. People tend to describe me as someone who's funny and who's kind. I've always joked that when I die, my epitaph will read *Here lies Jen; she was . . . nice.* To many people—readers, friends, and even family—I almost always appear to have it together. I tend to be a fixer, able to read other people and take care of their problems. I'm a listener. After all, that's why psychology seemed like such a good fit for me when I was in college. Most see me as laid-back and pretty much a happy person. And I know some might even think what do I have to be depressed over? I have a pretty successful career, great family, and tons of friends.

But I'm that headline.

You know the one. When the last person you'd ever expect commits suicide. The one person no one who knew

26

them saw it coming. There were no obvious signs or warnings. *That* headline. That could've been me. That could *still* be me. And it took me a long, long time to recognize that that not-quite-right part about me—that part of me that feels wired incorrectly and maybe a little broken—is truly a part of me. It took what felt like forever to learn that there are warning signs for me, at least ones that I can recognize.

My depression is usually driven by stress, and I tend to handle stress pretty decently—with the exception of randomly stringing together many variations of the f-bomb on any given day—but sometimes it builds up and up until all my muscles are tensed and I can't remember the last time I smiled. When it gets to that point, my old toxic friend rears its head, walks right through the front door uninvited with all its baggage.

And it hit me pretty hard at the 2016 RT Booklovers Convention. The stress-fueled depression had been building for several months, and everything came together all at once, forming the most messed-up storm possible. Lying in bed that Thursday morning, a few hundred feet from my friends, authors, and readers, I didn't want to do *it* anymore, do *anything* anymore. Feeling like there was something broken in my head once more, I was thinking about the Escape Clause. And God, I was really thinking about it. My mind racing over the different ways and the possibilities and the quiet, oh man, the *quiet*, because my head is never truly quiet, and I broke down like an angry toddler who had her cake taken away from her.

It's hard to put into words how it feels to be truly considering ending your life. I guess you could say it's surreal, but at the same time it almost feels too real. Everything is numb and oversensitive at the same time. Things are too bright, too dark, too loud, and too quiet.

I was at that point, had been at that point, on and off for months, and no one, not a single person around me knew.

But I didn't want to be that *headline*.

I didn't want to use the Escape Clause, because I had opted out once before, when I was seventeen.

Almost two decades later, I can't even recall all the details that drove my suicide attempt. Whatever had happened to me or how badly I had felt, turned out, decades later, to be so insignificant that I cannot truly remember why I decided my life wasn't worth living. Trust me, when people say whatever problems seem so big today are nothing years from now, they aren't lying. It's so true. What felt like *forever* to me back then is a *big nothing* now, but what has stayed with me all these years, like a damn shadow that follows me even when the lights go out, was what happened the very second I finished swallowing the last mouthful of pills. The very first thought that had erupted after I placed the plastic cup on my dresser.

I don't want to die.

I can still remember the bitter taste of pills and the even more acidic burn of panic. *What did I just do? What did I just do? What did I just do?* That question was on repeat, playing over and over. *Oh my God, what did I just do?* I knew immediately that I had chosen the wrong option.

I still remember the instantaneous regret I felt.

And that regret has stayed with me.

The difference this time? I didn't keep quiet. I told my friend something that was hard to say out loud and still is. Friday night, sitting in my hotel room, I told her I was having terrible thoughts. When I was seventeen, I hadn't told anyone. Not until it was almost too late.

And the Escape Clause is too late. For the most part, everything in life is fixable, but the Escape Clause isn't. You can't take back ending your life. You don't get a do-over. You don't get to experience the regret.

I'd been extremely lucky that it hadn't worked and I got a second chance. That doesn't mean I don't still struggle with depression and those terrible, dark, and insidious thoughts. That doesn't mean I don't still have a hard time opening up to anyone about these things.

Writing this essay is possibly one of the hardest things for me to do. I almost wish I couldn't put my name to it. It's not shame or guilt driving. I am a private person, so sharing something like this isn't the norm for me. But I think about the seventeen-year-old me, and I think about all the others who deal with depression in silence. I think about the stigma and ignorance surrounding depression that still persist to this day. I think about the fact I know I'm not the only one who lives with the Escape Clause in the back of their thoughts.

I know I'm not the only one who feels a little broken from time to time.

Those things are the reason why I agreed to do this, to attach my name to something so private and personal. Opening up about this is terrifying, but even as cliché as this sounds, if my experiences help one single person know they're not alone, know that the hundred voices screaming on Twitter or in real life aren't always right, then it was worth it. If one person chooses to not use the Escape Clause, then it was worth it. It will always be worth it.

Life is always a work in progress, and it is always worth living.

Twins

by
Amy
Reed

My addiction and depression are twins. They were born together. They have the same source, the same tangle of trauma, silence, chemistry, and blood.

The official term for this is "co-occurring disorder," or "dual diagnosis." There are all kinds of sciencey things I could tell you about this. But I am a storyteller, not a scientist. So I will tell you my story.

The year I turned thirteen was the worst year of my life. I was not ready for my beauty, not ready to be seen as something besides a little girl. Not ready for a new school, drugs, and a sociopathic bully. Not ready for another new school a few months later, not ready for more drugs, not ready for sex I did not fully consent to. Certainly not ready to navigate these terrors alone, with parents who looked the other way.

The first time I got high was the first time I forgot to be scared. I was barely thirteen. The second time I got high, I did it by myself. I felt safe. I had discovered something that gave me the power to control my feelings.

From the beginning, I loved getting high alone. Somewhere inside, I knew it was not normal for a thirteen-year-old to enjoy this so much. But I did not care. Secrets came naturally to me. I had been keeping myself a secret since before I can remember.

The next year, another new school. It was supposed to be a new beginning, but, of course, I was still the same person. I was only half there. I knew I was supposed to be making new friends, but I couldn't remember how to smile. I could barely speak. I was trailed by secrets, weighed down by trauma I had no tools to process. It was the early nineties. No one talked about PTSD back then, especially for pretty middle-class girls who got straight As and were so good at keeping secrets.

This was also before anyone talked about cutting or self-harm. I thought it was something I invented. I thought I was the only one in the world doing it. I'd sit alone in my room at night, holding a sewing needle or safety pin in a candle flame until it turned red hot. I'd burn holes in my arms until that single bull's-eye of pain was the only thing I could feel. The heavy burden of my emotions would evaporate in those moments. But of course they always came back.

In eighth grade I started carrying a dull pocketknife around with me. I'd sit on the floor of my bathroom next to a full bathtub, afraid to get in, afraid to go through with my plan. I'd hold the blade against my wrist and watch the indent it made as I pressed. I'd do this for hours. But I never pushed hard enough.

I don't know if I ever really wanted to die. I don't know if I wanted permanence. What I know is I wanted to stop feeling. I wanted an escape from myself. Drugs and self-harm had dulled the pain for a year or so, but by the time I was fourteen and at my fourth middle school, nothing I did could keep the feelings away.

I saw two options: die or ask for help. Dying wasn't working. Something wouldn't let me push the blade of that pocketknife in. I had an instinct to pull away from the darkness, some deep drive for self-preservation that led me back to life.

So I asked for help. I wish I could remember how this happened. I wish I had a blueprint or step-by-step instructions, a list I could make copies of and give away to everyone in pain. *This is how to ask for help*, it would say. This is how to tell your mom you need to talk to a doctor. This is how to not die.

But I do not have those instructions. I honestly do not remember. I have lost the important details. Those days are a weird blur of pain and numbness, punctuated by dull memories without context, memories of uncontrollable crying and then a blanket of cold detachment, memories of metal pressing on my wrist but not going in. And then I was in a doctor's office. Then I was in a therapist's office. Then I was in a psychiatrist's office. Then I had a bottle of pills that was supposed to cure me. This was still the early nineties. Prozac was all the rage.

What I remember was the thrill of excitement when I put

that first pill in my mouth. I finally felt a glimmer of hope. I felt the thrill of trying a new drug, the thrill of thinking I was going to feel a new high.

What I didn't know then is that antidepressants aren't supposed to make you feel high. They're supposed to help you feel closer to normal, help you stay in the gray area of emotion instead of spiking too far into blacks and whites. They often take weeks to start working, and the effect is so subtle you often don't notice it. They don't fix everything instantly. They don't put back together everything that's been broken. They change chemistry, but they don't change history. They do not dissolve memories.

But antidepressants saved my life. I didn't want to die anymore. My brain stopped its obsessive spiral to that particular dark place, but even with that chemical shift, I was still me. There are so many other kinds of darkness besides suicide, and the only thing I ever knew how to want was oblivion. So I kept looking for it.

What happened next was a decade and a half of more of the same, an escalating dance of highs and lows, from feeling too much to feeling nothing. Antidepressants evened me out, but I added drama with my own chemical concoctions. I was either chasing a high or running from a low. I was a hamster on a burning wheel. So much in my life was outside my control—my family, my body, my history, my feelings. Doing drugs made me feel, for the first time, like I was in control of something. I could turn my feelings on and off. I could even manufacture new ones.

The effects of drugs and alcohol were always different for me than for my friends. I seemed to always get higher and drunker than everyone else. I got sicker. I threw up and passed out more often. They knew when to stop, but I didn't. They could take it or leave it, but I couldn't.

Same with emotions in general. Someone else could brush off something that would send me into an emotional tailspin. Pain and suffering seemed to stick to me longer and harder than everyone else. My feelings were magnified to ridiculous proportions. I do not know if my feelings were actually bigger than everyone else's, or if I just lacked the coping skills that they all seemed to have. Regardless, feelings for me were dangerous, explosive things. They were out of my control. I did not trust them.

This was my dance of self-medicating: When emotional pain got bad, I drank and used more. When the pain of using got too much, I'd get clean for a while. But that temporary sobriety made room for the feelings to come back, and depression and anxiety would rush in to fill up the vacuum because I had no emotional tools to deal with the feelings. So I'd start using again to push the feelings back out. Sometimes I was on medication; sometimes I wasn't. Sometimes it didn't even matter since I was so full of other, stronger chemicals telling my brain what to do.

This pattern of running, of jumping between pains, was the only way I knew how to live.

I was sixteen years old the first time I went to rehab. They doubled my dose of antidepressants as soon as I got there. I didn't feel anything for nearly two years, which was just fine with me. I changed schools again and took most of my classes at a local community college because I couldn't bear to be a part of the normal high school world. I had very few friends, but they were good and loyal, and they are still some of my best friends today. I graduated early and worked at a gas station and a summer camp before going off to college. I was clean for almost two years, but it was a dark and lonely time.

I wish I were one of those people who loved college, who met the best friends of my life there, who goes to reunions and waxes nostalgic and wears my alma mater's T-shirt when I work out. But the truth is the two years I spent at that prestigious liberal arts college were two of the worst years of my life. It was the first time school was ever hard for me, and that crushed what little self-esteem I possessed. I had my first severe panic attack freshman year, when I couldn't leave my dorm room for two days and had to call a psychiatric crisis line. Most days I was high from the moment I woke up until I passed out at night. I locked myself in my room and played Elliott Smith and was terrified of everyone. My sophomore-year solution to the freshman fifteen was a handy new eating disorder that caused me to faint whenever I stood up too fast. I slept with people I did not like. I barely liked the few friends I had. I hated myself.

A few weeks before the end of sophomore year, I woke up one morning after a weeklong drug binge, got in my car, and drove home from Portland to Seattle. I hadn't been to class in days. I had hardly left my attic room in the house I shared with people I barely talked to anymore. My nose was in such bad shape, I had to start smoking things I had only ever snorted. I couldn't remember the last time I ate. I was out of money. I had destroyed everything.

For a long time I told myself I had had a nervous breakdown. I lived with my mom and started psychoanalysis three days a week but told neither my mother nor my analyst—or myself, really—about the role my addiction took in my decision to leave college. I worked part-time at a coffee shop. I hung out with old high school friends. I got my medication back on track after letting it slide while I was in college. But I was restless. I was mostly clean, but nothing was really changing. The style of analysis I was doing kept me in my head, away from all the painful feelings I was refusing to deal with. I was thinking about myself all the time, but I wasn't actually dealing with anything.

So what'd I do? I decided to move, of course. Running away from my problems had always worked so well for me in the past (insert sarcasm here). A couple of my buddies and I packed up a U-Haul and drove to San Francisco with no plan, no jobs, and no permanent housing. All I knew was that my dreams of being some kind of professional intellectual had been officially squashed. All I knew was I didn't want to live in my mom's basement anymore. All I knew was I had to run.

I turned twenty-one soon after I got to San Francisco.

That's when I learned how to *really* drink and found my true love of alcohol.

I was in my early twenties, living in San Francisco, and dating a bartender who loved to party. I worked in the service industry. I was studying film at a second-rate art school because I was too scared to try real college again. I made my world very small. It consisted of about two and a half neighborhoods in San Francisco and a handful of my favorite bars. I quit taking my medication because it interfered with my drinking.

This is what being young and fabulous in San Francisco looked like for me: Most nights I slept with a trash can next to the bed in case I puked. There was a week I couldn't leave the house because I had an anxiety attack every time I stepped out the door. I was constantly calling my girlfriend at work in a panic because I thought I was overdosing (at home getting high by myself while she worked late nights at the bar).

After a couple of years, my relationship fell apart, as most relationships built on partying do. I moved into a roach-infested studio apartment I could barely afford with my measly waitressing income. I finished school and met a nice boy who let me move in with him across the bay in Oakland. We had only been dating for a couple of months. That was twelve years ago. That boy is now my husband. Needless to say, he has put up with a lot.

I left the part of my life where the worst drugs and most trouble happened. I ran away again, but alcohol followed me to my new life. I got drunk nearly every night, whether I was with people or not. Depression and anxiety followed me too. For a while, I started cutting again, after not doing any kind of self-harm since my early teens. I cried myself to sleep sometimes, wailing into the night waiting for my partner to comfort me. But mostly, I drank until the pain stopped.

Over time things started to slowly change. In my new setting of Oakland, with my loving and patient partner and a growing new community of friends, I started putting myself back together. Therapy was working. Medication was working. I started jogging and doing yoga. I started writing again and got back some of that self-esteem I had lost in college. I started an MFA program and began work on what would become my first novel, *Beautiful*. I got a job in publishing. I got married. We adopted a dog. We bought a house. On the outside, everything looked perfect.

But I was still drinking almost every night. If I wasn't drinking, I was obsessing about it. I was still terrified of feelings, terrified of myself. Most of all, I was tired. I felt like I was working so hard but getting nowhere.

The thing about the disease of addiction is that it still progresses even if you're doing everything else right. For people with co-occurring mental illness and addiction, both diseases need to be treated. Despite all the hard work I was doing around my depression, anxiety, and trauma, I would never get well until I got honest with myself and did something about my alcoholism.

I knew it was my drinking that was holding me back. For a year I tried everything I could think of to cut down. I did cleanses and read self-help books. I made rules for myself, but I could not follow them. I made promises, but I broke them all. I tried quitting on my own, but the longest I lasted was two months. That year of failures left me demoralized. I knew I was powerless over alcohol and drugs. I knew I could not do it alone.

I was twenty-nine the second time I went to rehab. This time I was ready. I was humble and I was exhausted and I was sick of running the show, sick of my half-assed solutions, sick of the way I'd been doing things for so long. I knew I needed help, and I was willing to do any and everything they told me. I was ready to surrender.

As I write this, I am thirty-six years old, and I have been clean and sober for seven years. I have published seven novels and a handful of short stories and essays. I have a loving husband and an amazing daughter and a beautiful home in a beautiful mountain town. I have a beautiful life on the outside, and usually on the inside, too.

But my work is not done. It will never be done.

For me, maintaining my sobriety and mental health is made up of a series of small decisions, a series of small steps. Those decisions and steps are infinite, many of them unconscious, many of them so small I barely know I'm making them. It's not like one day I decided to be sober and everything changed. It is not like I decided to go on antidepressants and was suddenly cured of all the ways my brain plays tricks on me. These were steps in the right direction, but there were, and are, more steps to take. If I stumble—which I do, which we all do—if I wander off the path, the next step I take must be back in the right direction.

That's it. Most of the time it's that simple. One step, then another, then another, and hopefully most of them are in the right direction, and then you find yourself miles from where you started and your world looks nothing like it did before.

Even in recovery, even after years of therapy and medication, there is still so much work to do. It is unending. It is forever. There are still layers of myself to unfold, still shadows to bring to the light. There are still hills to climb, still plateaus to reach, still steps to take, still leaps to make it to the next phase of my journey.

And now, after so many steps, this is where I am:

I am thirty-six, and I do not know who I am without chemicals. From the age of thirteen, I have been on a nonstop combination of drugs, alcohol, and/or antidepressants.

I want to know who I am without them.

I recently decided, with the help of professionals, to taper off my medication. Not because I thought the meds were hurting me, but because I was curious. I consulted my medical doctor. I am seeing a therapist regularly. I am continuing work on my recovery and am involved in a recovery community. I run twenty miles a week and take a ton of brain-supporting vitamins. I try to eat healthy and sleep eight hours a night. I am checking in with friends, family, and professionals about my moods.

This is not a decision I take lightly. It is not a decision I think anyone else should or shouldn't make. It is mine and only mine. It is the right decision for me at this time in my life. I have been sober and emotionally and mentally stable for a long time. I feel safe and supported. I am in a good place to embark on this new journey.

But I am open to discovering it was not the right decision. I am open to the possibility of needing medication again. I am open to it not working.

I feel raw again, like I did when I was newly sober. I won't lie—these past few months have been difficult as my body and mind have been struggling through withdrawal and working tirelessly to find a new equilibrium. Like any medication, if an antidepressant is taken for a long period of time, the body and brain get used to it, and stopping, even with a slow taper as I have done, can be difficult for some people (but not everybody) because the body is trying to recalibrate without the medication.

At the beginning of my tapering down in dosage, I dealt with a series of panic attacks so physically intense I thought my heart was failing. I had a couple of weeks when I was full of rage nonstop. I had crying jags I thought I'd never come out of. I locked myself in the closet because the world hurt too much. I had mood swings so extreme I felt like a completely different person over the course of a few minutes.

I want to make something very clear: Antidepressants saved my life. I will never regret taking them. If you are in pain, if you need help, they may be the right answer for you. You should feel no shame in needing medication. This story of my withdrawal should not scare you away. These few short months of adjustment are a small price to pay for my life. Your life is worth whatever it takes to keep it.

I am surviving this period of adjustment. I am making it through these emotional spikes and, as time goes on, they are lessening in frequency and intensity. They've been countered by feelings on the other side—a new intensity of joy when I am doing things I love, a deeper feeling of connection with the people I share my life with, and a new dedication to change and to do the hard work of growing up and living with integrity. I am finding equilibrium.

After everything I've gone through, after all my pain and struggle, all my growth and triumph, I'm still an emotional baby. I'm still learning how to feel. I'm learning how to not run away. Being off antidepressants has lifted a veil, and I am experiencing a whole new layer of myself and the world around me. So many things I learned in early sobriety are coming back to me, so many tools I forgot I had and that I now need again.

I know how to ask for help now. I know how to reach out and tell people what's going on with me. I know I cannot keep everything inside, cannot let it fester and grow and feed on itself the way I did when I was young. Most of the time I can identify my toxic thoughts and stop the cycle of obsession before it destroys me. But it is still a struggle. It will probably always be a struggle. I accept this. I have to.

In early sobriety, when my body and mind were racked with cravings, I learned to create space between my thoughts and actions. So much about being an alcoholic and addict is wanting instant gratification, instant relief. It is in my nature to be unable to sit with discomfort and pain. There is nothing more excruciating than craving, and not just for addicts. Craving, yearning, wanting—they are part of the human condition.

But just because something's in our nature doesn't mean it can't change. Nature changes all the time. It's called evolution.

I have learned to wait. I have learned that thinking and feeling something does not mean I need to act immediately. I do not need to react. I can pause and check in with myself, ask myself what it is I really need. I can even set a timer—three minutes, five minutes—and when it rings, I usually find that that initial feeling, the sometimes desperate need to change how I'm feeling, has dissipated. After those few short minutes, I'm in a better place to make a decision.

Thankfully, I do not struggle these days with cravings for drugs and alcohol. But I still am, and always will be, an alcoholic and a drug addict. It is how my brain works. It feeds on my tendencies toward depression, anxiety, and obsession, requiring me to be constantly vigilant. Every struggle reminds me to stay mindful. Every craving for sugar or Netflix binges, every obsession, every grasping of something I can't control, reminds me I cannot be complacent. I cannot take my life for granted.

"Mindfulness" is the hip thing in mental health right now, and like most hip things, I have a natural distrust of it, even though I know it is a good idea. At the suggestion of countless friends and therapists, I've tried to develop a traditional meditation practice many times, but it's never stuck. I may never be someone who can sit still for thirty minutes every day and watch my thoughts float by like clouds the way I'm supposed to. But I can do small things. I can invite mindfulness into the moments of my life when I need to pause, when I need those three or five minutes between thinking/feeling/wanting/obsessing and making a choice. I can create the space that keeps an obsession from becoming a compulsive act. I can be brave and actually feel a feeling instead of trying desperately to push it away.

One thing I know for sure is that emotions get stronger the more I try to avoid them. Fighting and running prolong the pain and make it bigger. What emotions want is to be felt, and only then can they find completion. Only then can they end. I will never see the other side of pain unless I am brave enough to walk through it.

The more I do this, the more I walk through pain, the more I learn that feelings are temporary. I begin to trust that they will not kill me. I begin to have faith that I will make it to the other side. Again and again, I have made it, and I will continue to make it. And every time I do, I get a little stronger for the next time. I gain a little more confidence. I become a little braver.

I wake up in the morning grateful that I want to get out of bed, that I am happy to hear the birds and see the sunlight poking through the curtains. I am grateful that I am not sick, grateful that I am not starting the day with shame and fear. Every morning I wake up choosing life.

Most mornings I wake up to the sound of my three-year-old daughter down the hall calling, "Mama." She is the world's cutest alarm clock.

My daughter has never seen me drunk or high. She has seen me scary-cry a couple of times, so bad I could not get off the floor, and this breaks my heart. But she was not scared. She does not fear emotions the way I always have, neither mine nor her own.

When she cries, I hold her and tell her she's safe. I do not try to shush her. I do not tell her to be quiet or keep it in or push it away. I tell her it's okay to cry. I tell her it's okay to be scared and sad and angry. I tell her it's okay to feel her feelings.

But I think she already knows this. At three, she is already so brave.

It is not she who needs reminding.

Emphasis on the C

by Aprilynne Pike

Two windows rolled down on the freeway. The cool, early summer air whips by my cheek, through my hair, and the world is fresh.

I jack my iPhone into the speakers, Lady Gaga pours into my ears, the faint thump of bass vibrates my thighs from beneath my seat, and the world is vibrant.

Hand surfs the air in waves—up and down—red Lexus, spoiler, good sound system, not bad for the Parentmobile, engine revs beneath one foot on the gas pedal, and the world is fast!

A black truck approaches from the other direction, across the cement divider that splits the blacktop in two, north and south, and it catches my eye. Why? Who knows, but I watch it approach, vaguely hypnotic.

If I yanked my wheel, hit the barrier at a forty-five-degree angle, would the car flip across it? Could I fly and spin and roll and get that truck? How far would the debris spatter? Do it. Do it now!

My heart pounds, and the wheel is slippery as sweat dampens my palms. I can't loosen my grip, knuckles white under drum-tight skin. My heartbeat is a crash in my head—louder by far than the percussion in the song. I suck air through a small O between my lips, and panic is a red circle pressing in on my vision from all sides.

The signal is on. I don't remember turning it on, but at least it's blinking the correct direction. Right, not left. I cut off the guy beside me and he honks, but he doesn't know. Doesn't understand. There's a break in the next lane; then I only have to wait a second for the right-most lane. The exit is too far, and my sight is already a pinprick circle of light fighting through the darkness. Fighting.

Like me.

I'm only down to thirty, but I stomp hard on the brake and swerve to the shoulder. Bump off the asphalt. A small cloud of dust as I come to a stop in the crispy yellow weeds. The stifling smell of dirt wafts into my window, and it smells like being buried alive.

Up! Up! Windows up. Muffle the sound of traffic and hide behind the tinting. Finally I can close my eyes and lean my forehead on the steering wheel. Tiny drops of sweat travel onto it from my brow. Drip from the black leather wheel cover onto the jeans covering my thighs.

My fingers go automatically to my throat, where they zone

in on my pulse. Racing. Like the blood wants to explode from my veins. I'm not taking my pulse. It's a million and twelve beats per minute, and, besides, it doesn't matter. I'm not taking my pulse; I'm reminding myself that I'm alive.

Safe, I shout in my head, trying to overwhelm the soundtrack still pulsing through my brain that urges me to stomp on the gas. Reenter traffic. I don't have to make the desire go away. Yet.

But I have to be louder.

And I have to be smart. My hands shake, but I shove the car into park and jerk the keys from the ignition. I start to toss them onto the passenger seat, but that's bowing to the voices. Even if only a little. I fling them way into the back seat instead.

And don't let myself look to see where they land.

OCD, my therapist said. Emphasis on the C.

It started a year ago. Right in the middle of a growth spurt. Changes and hormones can sometimes trigger its unveiling, she said. Changes in the body, when the mind longs for stability, she said.

She said a lot of things. A lot of smart things. But knowing the why doesn't help when you're standing in the middle of an overpass, gripping the edge of the concrete railing so hard that later you have scabs on your fingertips and left eight little maroon circles on the white cement.

I wanted to jump. *Needed* to jump.

I'm not suicidal. It's hard to explain. I like my life. I want to live. I get better-than-average grades, do debate, track and field, and play trumpet in pep band. I'm dating an awesome person, and we don't fight. I want to go to college. And before that, I want to have a great senior year. People seem to like me; I'm not gorgeous or anything, but I look pretty good. There's nothing *wrong* with my life.

But a year ago I wanted to jump. My brain played over and over the sight of my skull bursting on the asphalt below, a perfect circle of blood and gore painting the street like artwork.

I've never wanted food or water or air or sex the way I wanted to see that art.

I cried. On that bridge. Begged myself not to want it. I honestly don't know how I got through it that day. Don't know why I'm alive. But I went home, and I was a mess.

Luckily, my mom and dad listened. Some don't. Many don't. I've learned that.

They didn't *understand*, and I don't blame them. I didn't understand either. I told them over and over that I didn't want to die; I just wanted to jump. Onto the pavement. Into oncoming traffic. Better if I could time it right and get hit by a semi on the way down. Who would understand that? It's just—

Crazy.

So they took me to a therapist. She was the one who helped me see the other episodes. Smaller ones that led up to the day at the bridge. Ones I hadn't thought of as compulsions at all. The urge to go shoulder-check the meanest football player in the school. Just to see if he'd hit me. If he broke my nose, would blood splatter the wall? Out on a hike with some friends, wondering if the little patch of mushrooms I saw was poisonous enough to kill me. How many I'd have to eat. Could I puke up my own organs?

The bridge episode was just the one big enough to get my attention. The first time that soundtrack got loud enough to drown out my own brain.

Meds, she said. Immediately. It's not the answer for everyone, she said as her pen scritch-scratched out the prescription. But your compulsions are destructive. Let's get them under control first, and then we'll start.

Start? I thought the meds would be the answer. The cure.

But there is no cure.

Still. They worked for me. They didn't make the compulsions go away, and they certainly didn't change them from making me want to somehow destroy myself. But they softened the soundtrack. Like turning music down from something that makes your head throb and ears bleed to something you only have to shout over to be heard.

I need that little bit. I'll probably always need it, though Dr. Simpkins says I might rethink that when I'm fully—physically—an adult. I'm not ready to look that far into the future.

Certainly not now, as I sit by the side of the road. A car honks as it passes, and it sounds the way a crescendo, then decrescendo, looks. A small sound that grows bigger and slaps you in the face before receding again as the vehicle drives away.

Stupid driver. Who honks at someone on the side of the road? He's probably an asshole. I should get my car back on the road and chasehimdownand—

"Safe, safe, safe," I whisper in time with my heartbeat. That urge wasn't a true compulsion. It's my brain being sneaky. Trying to get me back on the road so it can hit me again. One-two. Right-left. Uppercut-cross. Knockout.

"Safe, safe, safe," I continue whisper-chanting. It's a coping mechanism that works for me. We've tried lots of things. "We" is me and Dr. Simpkins. An army of two. Even when we find something that works, we keep trying things.

Coping mechanisms, for any mental illness, are very personal, she said when I complained. What works for you won't work for someone else. And vice versa. And sadly, what works today might not work tomorrow, she said. So we try lots of things. *Stocking the arsenal,* she calls it.

Weapons for a fight. Because, for me at least, it is a fight. A life-and-death fight.

And despite what my brain wants to tell me, I don't want to die.

I have some hard and fast rules: I avoid bridges. If I have to cross a bridge, I walk in the middle and look neither left nor right. And I try not to be alone. Tops of buildings? No. I didn't drive for six months. At all. Not until I felt ready. And even though you get super strapped in, roller coasters are simply not a good idea for me. Feeds the troll, so to speak.

It doesn't stop it from happening; it just keeps me from

giving my brain a better chance. A deeper toehold. Like an alcoholic avoiding bars, I avoid places of danger no normal person thinks of as dangerous.

Avoidance. Before *and* after. Get off the road; get away from the power saw; turn your back on the bonfire.

Once I tried holding still instead of running away. On the edge of the temptation. Dr. Simpkins said a lot of people use that strategy. Stop. Resist. And then feel victorious when you can.

It doesn't make me feel victorious. It makes me feel worse. More broken. My brain already latches on to how broken I feel. Taunts me with it. I tried it, like she said. I tried. But it made everything worse, and I'm glad my friend Jenna was with me that day to pull me away when she saw that look in my eye.

I'm glad I told her.

I didn't tell very many people. It makes me feel dirty sharing how messed-up my brain is. And that goes back to remembering how broken I am, and the cycle starts again, growing bigger each trip around the block until I can't hear anything but my mind shouting at me like a skipping record. Wrong, broken, *wrong, broken, Wrong, Broken, WRONG, BROKEN.* And I still don't know how to turn that volume down.

Jenna grabbed my arm and pulled me away. She says I dug my feet into the sand and she had to yank on my arm, and still I stared at the fire that a bunch of the guys were jumping over.

I wanted to jump too.

Not over. *In.* To roll in the red coals until my skin was

charred and it broke and oozed like meat on a spit. I didn't tell Jenna that, exactly. I don't tell anyone those details except Dr. Simpkins. I don't tell them how my brain thinks such destruction has the ethereal beauty of a fine painting.

Avoidance. I live to run away another day, and I'm not ashamed of that. I *want* to live. I don't know why my brain wants to paint with my blood. Shoves at me from the inside. Pushes me forward like a physical force.

When that shove comes, my meds help me stand still, but it's up to me to force myself to take a step back. That is my fight. Every day. I don't have an episode every day. Not even every week. Maybe I'd be better at it if I did—you know what they say about practice—but maybe perfection is overrated.

I breathe in and out with my fingers at my throat, and after a few more minutes I can sit back, lean my head against the headrest, and breathe through my nose. I don't open my eyes. Not until I'm certain the tunnel vision is gone.

I count. A bit of that O slipping in, but I can use it as a tool. Like using your enemy's own weapon against them. One hundred breaths. Two hundred. Three hundred. In. Out. In. Out. *One, safe. Two, safe. Three, safe.*

I once tried thinking about reasons to live, but it only made it take longer. For me, it was pointless. Because I don't want to die. I just want to do things that would make me die. It doesn't matter that it doesn't make sense. If it made sense, it would be easy to fix.

The whole point is that it doesn't make sense.

I crack my eyelids after six hundred breaths. I thought I was ready at five hundred, so I made myself count to six. Another trick.

A glance down at my phone. It took just over half an hour. This was a bad episode. And the aftereffects will linger for days. Wanting to hate myself, picking the whole episode apart and analyzing what I did wrong, what I could have done better. But I beat it. Beat the worst moment. This time. Every victory is the most important. At least until the next one. Then that one becomes most important.

But I'm ready again. The compulsion is a hum of background music now, instead of a head-splitting scream. I can return to the world.

Once I finally find them, I have to practically contort my body to grab my keys, far away on the floor behind the passenger seat, where they tumbled out of sight. Which was the point.

I start the car.

Two windows roll back down. Gusts of air from the cars rushing past curl under my sunglasses, cooling red-rimmed eyes, and the world is bearable.

I jack my iPhone into the speaker, Frank Sinatra croons an oldie, the violins are a bright tang in my eardrum, his voice a softer baritone coating, and the world is sharp.

The click of my signal, brake, lean on the gas, tires spin in the gravel, kicking up pebbles, crunch onto the pavement as the force of my acceleration glues me to my seat, and I am alive for another day.

I Am Not This

by Rachel M. Wilson

A family portrait:

I'm visiting the fam over the summer, and it's eleven p.m. on the night before a weeklong beach vacation. Dad's instructed everyone to be ready to go bright and early. "Let's all set our alarms for eight a.m.!" Mom says optimistically.

Dad tears around the house adjusting timers on lights to ward off burglars, gathering camera equipment that he rarely uses but *might* regret leaving behind. "For once, we're getting out ahead of traffic," he says. We *ought* to be leaving by seven a.m., but even we champions of denial can't pretend that's attainable. We've settled on a more believable nine. "If you're not ready by then," Dad lies, "we're leaving without you."

My parents stay up late, packing and fretting and trying to eliminate last-minute distractions. Dad checks the weather, weighing the predictions of rain against the plants' need for water. Mom vacuums so she won't be tempted to do it in the morning. By the time I go to bed, well after midnight, Dad's just pulling down the attic stairs to fetch suitcases.

My mother wakes me with a cheery knock on the door around nine thirty. No one acknowledges that I never set an alarm. No one expected me to. Our collective ability to share in the fiction of how the morning might go, while individually admitting there's no hope for us, points to superpowers of cooperative denial and self-delusion that must have some positive application in this world. Unfortunately, our family's particular heroic calling has yet to be discovered, and year after year, the seemingly straightforward task of leaving town Kryptonitically wears us down.

Any minute we'll be on our way . . . at 10:26, 11:14, 11:52. Any. Minute. Now.

By 12:08 p.m., the car is packed, but Dad's scrubbing the grout in the shower or watering the shrubbery. Mom is eating a leisurely breakfast. My sister and I watch TV because no one's actually going to be ready for another hour. Every fifteen minutes or so, one of my parents harangues us to get a move on. We promise we're ready; let us know when you are.

Flash forward to the truly last minute, 12:24 or 12:58 or 1:02 . . . Dad's saying next time we'll drop the dogs off for boarding the night before, and that will solve all our woes. Mom's asking does anyone need a Dasani for the ride because she's getting herself a Dasani and even if they are just water, they're delicious. My sister's sitting stoically in the back seat, hands tucked under her arms, earbuds in, where she's *been* sitting, in a patient demonstration of martyrdom, for the past hour. As Dad fusses to find the perfect balance between open and closed shutters, I'm in the bathroom doing my makeup because no one gave any indication of being ready for the past five hours, and now it's suddenly time to go? My mom and sister take bets on whether my father or I will make it to the car first.

If we make it out of town without having to go back for something, it will be a minor miracle.

My sister (at the time) is the only one of us with an actual diagnosis of ADHD. My sister is the only one taking medicine. My sister is the only one who's been ready to leave since waking.

I recently learned that roughly 30 percent of people with OCD (which I've had since age ten) also have ADHD.

People with high IQs and creative types are more likely to have it. I fall into both of those categories.

My sister has ADHD, and it runs in families.

For decades my family has taken it for granted that my dad has undiagnosed ADHD, with an emphasis on the *H* for hyperactivity. As a baby, Dad used to rock his crib across the floor by inches. He broke his mother's rib from flailing. He slept with a hammer—his "hammy"—which made lots of noise when it wasn't asleep. As a teenager, his antics got him shipped off to military school. He can focus for hours on things that interest him—yard work, carpentry, photography—but he needs to be building, moving, doing.

Our house rule is "make sure you have eye contact" before speaking . . . to anyone, but especially to my father and me. We can be in the same room as you, three feet away, and not hear you calling our names.

My mom lives in her own space-time continuum, wherein travel does not cost time. For years I assumed I had inherited my slippery relationship with time from her. She can be orderly, but some corner of the home is always toppling toward chaos. I see my own housekeeping fails as an exaggeration of those cluttered corners. Maintenance and routine don't come easily to me. My natural inclinations are to let the world burn and then restore order in one furious, phoenixlike cleaning binge. Often my energy for that herculean task peters out before it's complete, leaving rooms worse than when I started.

Obviously I can't diagnose either of my parents with ADHD, but I think it's fair to call us an ADHD family.

So how did I make it to 2015 without realizing I had ADHD?

The key, I think, is that my ADHD doesn't look like the ADHD I learned about growing up. More on keys later . . .

I grew up believing that people with ADHD always struggle in school and that they're always hyperactive. I thought most kids who had it were boys and that all people with it were kids, that ADHD was something to be outgrown.

I, on the other hand, had an easy time in school. I thrived in the transparently named "gold" reading group, was chosen for special pullouts and academic teams. Far from being hyperactive, I was prone to deep focus and an eerie stillness when lost in thought—a classic sign of the predominantly inattentive type of ADHD.

Looking back, there were other signs. . . . Growing up, I was notorious for a staggering obliviousness to my surroundings. My parents could rearrange the furniture, buy a new painting, tear down a wall, and I wouldn't notice. Often the change had to be pointed out to me.

I preferred the company of adults when I was in preschool. The noise and motion of the other kids threw me off-balance. I told my pediatrician that they gave me headaches. At three I enforced silent reading time during the carpool to school. In elementary school I'd often become so absorbed in a book that I'd bring it to the lunch table and prop it up around my plate like a shield. When another kid asked, "Why do you stare into space all the time?" I'd answer, "I'm just thinking."

My oddities were blamed on high intelligence and creativity—great problems to have—and, when I was older, on my OCD. Obsessive thinking and problems with attention can be hard to distinguish, and an OCD streak of perfectionism can mask ADHD's careless mistakes and unfinished projects. In my *non*academic life, no one forced me to focus on the boring stuff. Partly *because* I did so well in school, my parents let me get away with a messy room. They let me do my homework in front of the TV. The background noise might have made it hard for a different kid to concentrate, but it calmed my mind down. I didn't know it at the time, but the TV was filling an ADHD need for constant stimulation.

Theater did the same thing for me. I loved the *drama*, the life-or-death stakes, and the adrenaline rush of performing. Many researchers associate the stimulation-seeking and hypervigilance of ADHD with the skills early human hunter-gatherers needed for survival. I'm great in a crisis, and there's nothing quite like high school theater for disasters waiting to happen. For six years I earned most of my income performing in simulations of medical emergencies for med schools. Yes, I got paid to pretend that someone (often myself) was about to die.

ADHD stands for attention deficit hyperactivity disorder, but those words can be misleading. An attention "deficit" doesn't refer to a *lack of* attention but to a difference in how attention functions. Many people with ADHD experience hyperfocus on one thing to the exclusion of all else. In school, hyperfocus was my superpower. When I'm really into what I'm doing, the outside world slips away. I'm immune to distraction, fully engaged, and time passes quickly. Downside: I won't hear you calling my name. I ignore the alarm that's supposed to snap me out of it. I might not notice if a fire starts.

Now, about those keys . . .

In college, for the first time, no one organized my life for me. My grades didn't suffer, but everything else did. My sleep suffered because I couldn't seem to care about writing a paper until the last minute. I'd pull all-nighters, coating my tongue with instant-coffee powder, and receive glowing comments from my professors. I did *all* the suggested reading—hundreds of pages a week. I'd routinely hear people say, "No one does *all* the reading," and I'd say, surprised, "Oh, I do." My immune system suffered—after a week of auditions or exams, I always came down with something. Eventually, I'd crack into crying jags and anxiety attacks. I once saw little red hearts swimming through the air in front of my professor, a hallucination brought on by stress and the start of a sinus infection. And in those moments of deep exhaustion, I'd forget my keys.

No keys meant no access to my books or computer until my roommate returned. I told myself that forgotten keys were my brain's way of begging for a break, so I'd take one, napping in the dorm suite's lounge.

After college, I became skilled at breaking and entering—into my own apartment. I enjoyed the challenge. I received a ticket for leaving my car running . . . with the keys locked inside. A well-worded indignant letter about the injustice of punishing taxpayers for simple mistakes got me out of paying.

But eventually my slips started wearing me down. I was always running late, everywhere. Sometimes my problem was inattention. I'd walk out the door without my bag and have to go back. Sometimes pushing up against boundaries did me in. It seemed like a waste of time to be early, and cutting it close meant running late. Other times, hyperfocus was the culprit. I once showed up to rehearsal twenty minutes late, holding an elaborately designed prop—an employee name tag—as my excuse. The prop made the scene funnier. For me, it *made* the scene. Was it worth being twenty minutes late? Of course not, because I could have made it at any other time. But in the moment of inspiration, as dumb as it sounds, that paper and plastic became my sun and stars. While I was making it, nothing else mattered.

I did better under stress, when there might be real consequences to being late, but if the pressure climbed too high, my internal stress-o-meter would snap and I'd give up on being early. I'd be shockingly late if that's what it took to destress the situation. *No one's going to die if I'm late,* I'd tell myself, but I guess I needed proof.

Chronic lateness became part of my identity, a part I didn't like.

And throughout my twenties, there were worse failures. On a family trip to France, I lost my passport and plane ticket. I'd never seen my parents so distraught because of something I'd done wrong. I wasn't used to doing *anything* wrong. "This would only happen to Rachel," my cousin said, and that took me by surprise. Was my life secretly a sitcom and I the only one who'd never noticed?

One morning when I was supposed to be performing in a children's theater show, I woke to five frantic messages. I'd missed an e-mail about an added show date. Someone had to stand in for me, holding a script, on the day the show was being filmed. As an overachiever and trouble avoider, knowing I'd let everyone down shattered me.

Two years into my first serious relationship, I sensed the end was near. We were fighting a lot, often over my continual failings—to shut a cabinet door, to be ready on time, to remember my phone/wallet/keys. In a single week I managed to lock my keys in the car with it running *three times*, twice in one day. Each time, my beleaguered boyfriend drove across town to bring me the spare set. Each time felt like one more nail in the coffin of our doomed relationship, and some part of me knew that was *why* it kept happening. My sense that things were on the verge of falling apart made me make things fall apart.

Years later, we were back together and on the rocks again. We went camping in Joshua Tree, a trip I'd planned because I never planned things. I hate *having* plans, much less making them, but I was trying. We were getting along, roasting marshmallows and talking about our future, when we returned to the car for some water. As I slammed the trunk closed, I realized I'd left the keys inside. I had never set the keys down inside the trunk before. I didn't remember doing it then. My brain had gone on autopilot and betrayed me, leaving us without access to our provisions in the wild desert dark. The boyfriend had to take a walk to cool down. *Well, that's it,* I thought. One slammed trunk, one decapitated relationship.

And of course, nothing's so simple. We survived—even enjoyed—the rest of the weekend. When the end came, it was mutual, inevitable, friendly even, and brought on by many factors, but I'd always link it to the sound of that trunk slamming. I couldn't help but wonder, if I'd had a better grip, might things have gone differently?

Several years and lots of lost keys later, I'd be crying in recognition over a book titled *It's Hard to Make a Difference When You Can't Find Your Keys*.

My problem has to do with Executive Function. I picture Ms. Function as a sharply dressed fast-talker, a CEO/card shark/daredevil who treats the hopes and dreams of lesser mortals as red carpet for her spike heels. Ms. Function works on the two thousandth floor and surveys her domain through half-lidded eyes. She deigns to visit me when I need her the most, when the world's burning down and the hydrants have run out of water. Ms. Function thrives on deadlines, near misses, close calls. She screams up in her adrenaline-fueled Lambo and hollers, "Get in!" With Ms. Function at the wheel, I can compose prizewinning papers in early morning twilight, act my way through a play with the flu, handle crises without breaking a sweat, go with my gut, and *know* that the world's on my side. And once Ms. Function's work here is done, she leaves me with an adrenaline crash and often a cold. It's taken me years to recognize that dragged-out, frayed exhaustion for what it is: the hangover from a string of days being wined and dined by the most daring, effective version of myself.

Most days I'm stuck with Dysfunction. She's a whimsical

gal with a crush on the slacker guitarist who lives in the basement. When it's time to make a decision or switch gears between tasks or remember to stop by the library, Dysfunction dons her hippie skirt and Birkenstocks from the eighth grade that she can't bear to get rid of and shows up unannounced. Dysfunction thinks now would be a great time to practice the ukulele she bought three years ago but never learned to play. When confronted with a decision between smartphone A and smartphone B, she paces, panic stricken. Dysfunction spends several hours a week over five months researching her options. My friends take bets on when I'll finally get it together to buy a new phone. Only the threat of a long car ride without one makes Ms. Function take the elevator down to make the choice, quick and sharp like the snapping of a bone.

When my mother first suggested I might have ADHD, I dismissed the idea, but the more self-help books I read, the more I thought about it. Years after she first brought it up, I read a blessed article in *The Atlantic* titled "ADHD Is Different for Women." It's one of several recent articles acknowledging that many women are being diagnosed for the first time as adults after years of struggle. Early ADHD research focused on hyperactive boys who had trouble in school, so no one realized that ADHD develops later in girls, that it doesn't always cause hyperactivity or bad grades, and that it sometimes gets worse rather than better with age. Girls and women with ADHD are more prone to depression and anxiety. We're apt to see this biological problem as a failure of character, and that's murder on the self-esteem. When you don't understand how your brain's letting you down, it is far too easy to internalize your symptoms, to see yourself as weak, lazy, or bad.

I am not those things, and neither are you.

In many ways, I'm a maven of order. I have to be. My Google calendar is a rainbow of time blocks. My inbox is sorted with stars and folders. Any time I leave the house, I use two alarms—one to let me know it's time to go and one to wake me from deep focus at least twenty minutes before. Unfortunately, when I'm under stress, these systems break down. I make mistakes. When that happens, I try to remember that I work harder than most people to be responsible and reliable, and that I usually succeed. I try to keep my sense of humor. I try to forgive myself.

Medicine helps—a lot—but it only works for hours at a time, and it can make my anxiety worse. Figuring out how it can best serve me is a learning curve.

I try to meditate daily. Mindfulness helps with attention *and* anxiety. When I'm overwhelmed and fed up with myself, I remember a phrase learned in yoga class. The teacher had us sitting back on our toes, a position that causes most people some tension and pain. To get through the stretch, she said, we were to repeat the Sanskrit words *neti, neti. I am not this. I am not this.* I am not this pain. I am not this body. I am not this brain.

When I'm bogged down by a failure of the organ that rests in my skull, when I'm hung out to dry by an imbalance in the chemical bath that's supposed to fuel it, when a power outage in the office of Ms. Function makes the struggle real, I remind myself I am not this brain. I am not this stream of neurotransmitters. I am not this lack of attention or this laser beam of focus. I am not a set of lost keys.

Neti, neti.

The Girl in the Kitchen

by Dan Wells

When my wife and I first got married, we lived with my grandfather because my grandma had just died and he needed someone to take care of him and the timing just kind of worked out. He needed live-in care because he had Alzheimer's, and I'd spent a significant portion of my childhood living with him anyway, so of course I volunteered. We stayed with him for eight months before our schedule forced us to move out, and it was one of the hardest eight months of my life. I kind of assumed that it was over when we moved, but no. Building your life around a crippling mental illness, even if it's not your own, is a thing that never leaves you. Every time I think I've got my head on straight again, something new will happen to bring those feelings back, and throw it all into shambles.

My grandparents kind of half raised me, not because my parents weren't there but because my grandparents always were. We had dinner at their house every Sunday, and often one or two days in between. I slept over at their house as often as not. When I started second grade, bussing across town to an elementary I couldn't walk to, they picked up my brother and me every day after school, sometimes driving us home, but just as often taking us to their house first, where we played or did homework or watched TV or did whatever. They came to every birthday, holiday, and school event I ever had; they taught me how to cook and clean and mow a lawn and weed a garden. My memories of spending time with them are almost certainly inflated—I can't possibly have spent as much time with them as I think I did—but in my mind those memories loom large. I loved my grandparents, and they loved me, and that love was one of the foundation stones my life was built on.

There were signs that my grandma also had some form of dementia, though we didn't really recognize it at the time. The early stages manifested primarily as mild paranoia, which is common enough, but mild paranoia by its nature is easy to hide: She thought people wanted to steal family heirlooms and other things, so she started hiding them around her house without telling us, and because she was good at hiding things, we never really noticed. Some of her more quirky eccentricities are easy to quantify, in hindsight, as hallucinations, which are another strong indicator of dementia, but at the time we just thought she was stressed. Grandpa was far more obviously senile, so he got the attention—we weren't really helping her; we were helping her take care of him. Symptoms aside, she was a rock, and she was amazing, and she passed away before she had a chance to really lose her mind. That was in early 1999, just a month or so before I got married, so my aunt moved in with Grandpa for a bit, and then she went home and my fiancée moved in with my grandpa, and then we got married and I moved in with them.

I was twenty-two years old, and it had been years since I'd slept over at his house, but it was comforting and familiar and unfamiliar and terrifying all at once. I'd known, academically, that he had strong dementia symptoms, but I had no idea the full extent of his degeneration.

I got my first sense of how much the experience of living with Alzheimer's had affected me several years later, watching a movie at home with my wife. The story was about two people who meet and fall in love and grow up and grow old and then one of them gets Alzheimer's, and fine, whatever. I spent most of the movie paying less attention to the love story than to the depiction of Alzheimer's, which felt off the whole time. I wasn't sure if this was because it was inaccurate to the disease or just to my experience of the disease, but it was definitely off. Alzheimer's is essentially a memory disease—it has several other symptoms, including some I've already mentioned, like paranoia and hallucinations, and some I haven't, like violence and anger—but at its core it's about the loss of memory. You see an object or a face, or you hear a voice or a song or a sound, and your brain looks for the file to tell you what it is and can't find it. The file is gone. You don't recognize people you've known your entire life, or you misidentify them, and then maybe the next day you'll remember them again, but you'll forget something else. It comes and it goes, and it often seems to target the most personal memories it can—you're unlikely to forget your favorite food, for example, but you'll absolutely forget the person who serves it to you.

So the movie goes on, and the guy keeps trying to get his wife to remember him, and then suddenly at the end the fog lifts, and she remembers everything: not just him, but everything, their entire life together, and they have a joyful, tearful reunion, and I completely melted down, sobbing on the couch, not because I was glad that they'd gotten together but because I was angry—completely furious—that Alzheimer's didn't actually work that way. It's not a switch that goes on and off. Some memories come back for a while, but never all of them, and never all at once. I was incensed, not because the movie was wrong, but because life itself was wrong. Because the reality of Alzheimer's was so much worse than the movie could possible depict.

Because I never got that joyful reunion with my grandfather. He forgot me, and he never remembered me again, and then he died.

My wife and I are both pretty centered, easygoing people, so living with my grandpa as caregivers was pretty simple for the first few weeks. He'd ask us who we were, usually several times a day, and we'd tell him, and we'd move on. He was a pretty easygoing guy as well, which helped a lot. One of my favorite stories is the time when he, sitting in the living room, looked over at my wife and said, "You know, that girl in the kitchen talks to herself," which I loved because the girl in the kitchen was my wife, who talks to herself all the time, and it felt like several different layers of unreality and perception were all washing up against each other in that one little sentence, and he was aware of some but not others. I don't know why that tickled me so much, but I loved it.

But time goes on, and Alzheimer's progresses, and proximity creates friction that slowly but surely starts wearing people down. We'd been there about a month the first time he locked me out—it was nighttime, and I needed to get something out of my car, so I went outside, and he raced to the door and locked and chained it. "Don't worry," he told my wife. "He can't get back in." She explained that she wanted me to get back in because I was her husband and she loved me. "That guy?" Yes. "Him?" Yes. He frowned at her: "You're not the kind of girl to go with a guy like that." She unlocked the door, and he grumbled and walked away, and half an hour later he'd forgotten the whole thing. My wife and I laughed about it, and I knew that it wasn't him who didn't like me—it was the disease. He wasn't himself. He wasn't thinking clearly. He didn't know who I was, and every other excuse I could think of. But . . . that doesn't really make it better, does it? He didn't know I was his grandson, sure, but he'd been talking to me just a few minutes earlier, and then he'd locked me out. Obviously I'd said something to bother him. Maybe I really was a horrible person, so bad that the wonderful man who raised me couldn't wait to get rid of me. Maybe the loss of memory enabled him to see me in a new light, with all the pretense ripped away, for who I really was. Maybe he'd always wanted to lock me outside, and Alzheimer's finally removed whatever inhibitions had been stopping him for so long.

None of this is true. Always remember that. My grandpa used to love me, and he still did, but his brain had betrayed him, and it was making him do things he would never do— would never dream of doing. I learned to think about the human brain as essentially a filter that receives all the inputs from the world around us, all the sights and sounds and smells and sensations, and then interprets them and tells us how to react. If that filter is damaged, then the inputs we receive are damaged as well, or incomplete, or blurred or fractured or tinted or altered, and our ability to process those inputs and choose a reaction to them is hindered. When you drive a car with broken mirrors, or a cracked or dirty windshield, then you can't see as much of the road, and even the best driver in the world is at a distinct disadvantage. If you look at a face, and your brain tells you it's not your grandson but some random hooligan intruding in your home, you react to a hooligan. My grandpa didn't hate me, or any of the other scenarios I'd concocted, and I had to learn to remember that. But Alzheimer's doesn't make it easy, even for the people who can remember things.

The first and only time I fought with my grandpa—literally

ever—was a few months later. We were trying to be the best caregivers we could be, but we also had our own lives to live and our own decisions to make, and those decisions were not always the ones my grandpa would have made in our place. It's not like we were out doing drugs or tattooing babies or anything. Our fight was about a candle. My wife put a scented candle in our bedroom, just to brighten up the place, and it drove him berserk. Having an open flame in the house bothered him to distraction: He fixated on it, convinced that it would light the entire home on fire the second he looked away. He put it out anytime he found it lit and shouted, "They're going to cancel our insurance!" if we ever dared to light it again. I tried to explain that it was innocuous—that we were being careful, that we'd put it in a good place, that we'd removed any flammable objects from the area—but nothing would satisfy him. The argument grew more heated. After so many compromises for him and his routines and his disease, for some reason this was the one that broke the camel's back; this was the one I took a stand on. I explained that no insurance company in the world would cancel your policy for a single candle flame; I explained that if candles were as dangerous as he seemed to think they were no one would even be allowed to make them; by the end of it we were shouting at each other, and I called him ridiculous, and he stormed off with a snarl. I stared at the candle and realized that I'd just yelled at my grandpa—not just fought with him but yelled at him. Over a stupid candle. I couldn't chalk this one up to Alzheimer's, because I was the one who'd done it. It was me. I put out the candle and put it away, and never got it out again. Grandpa forgot the whole thing within half an hour, as always, but I never did, and I never will.

Just as having a mental illness changes your perception of the world, living with someone else's illness changes your perception of yourself. You learn more about who you are and what you want and what you're capable of doing than you ever knew before. And a lot of that stuff is not going to be good. It's harder than you think it is, and more draining, and it never ends, because these diseases don't get cured—they get managed. It might be easier some days than others, and with good medication and therapy it might seem to an outsider that the problem is gone altogether, but it's always there, and you always have to deal with it, and you want to do it because you love them, but that doesn't make it any less tiring or painful or hard.

I wrote a book about memory—a monster who eats other people's memories in order to sustain his own—and I knew that my experience with Alzheimer's would help inform that writing, but I wasn't ready for the flood of emotions that came rushing out onto the page. It was like opening a tap that breaks, and water is gushing everywhere and there's nothing you can do to stop it, and here I was with a horror story about monsters and hunters and cannibals and serial killers, and the most terrifying thing in it, by a mile, was the relentless entropy of memory loss. The characters could struggle to stay ahead of it, but it was always going to get them in the end. I had to tone it way down to make it work in the book. But I wanted to leave as much of it as possible in there, because it's a truth that needs to be told. Painful truths usually are. Stories that gloss over it, like the movie I watched, give us the false hope that our problems can go away if we try hard enough, but that's not how the world works, and it's not how we should work. I didn't take care of my grandpa through all the problems and hardships and obstacles because I thought he might come out of it in the end; I took care of him because I loved him and he needed help, and there were no false resolutions of magical cures. There are bad times, and they will never go away, but there are good times too, and they never go away either.

Sometimes you get locked out. But sometimes that girl in the kitchen talks to herself. And it doesn't make sense, but it does make it worth it.

Therapy: The Gift I Give Myself

by Amber Benson

I have a slightly unique view of mental health because I grew up with two parents who worked in the field. My dad is a psychiatrist, and my mom is a psychiatric nurse with an undergraduate degree in psychology. When I was a kid, my dad had a private practice in Birmingham, Alabama, that he and my mom ran together. My sister and I spent a lot of time there after school and on the weekends, and I have fond memories of playing office—with the massive IBM electric typewriter, the Xerox copier, and about a thousand office supplies—while my mom worked in the front office and my dad saw patients.

Back then I thought that someone having mental health problems was no different from someone who was having physical "body" problems—and this is still my point of view. I didn't, and still don't, see the difference. I knew my dad was a doctor who helped people—kind of in the same way my pediatrician helped me when I was sick—but unlike my pediatrician, who looked in ears, noses, and throats, my dad looked into people's minds.

My dad was a physician for over fifty years (he only retired recently), and I know that in those five decades he was responsible for helping many, many people—the majority of whom went on to lead successful and fulfilling lives, despite battling mental illness each and every day. He was of the mind that therapy could have a profound effect on a patient, and if you coupled that therapy with the proper psychiatric drugs (when necessary), you could have a lot of success.

He taught me the brain is just an organ like any other. No different from the heart or the kidneys or the liver. That a psychiatrist treats chemical imbalances in the brain the same way other doctors treat chronic illness in the body: with proper medical monitoring and medication.

I mean, a diabetic takes insulin. An epileptic takes anti-seizure medication . . . so why is a person stigmatized for taking a drug that helps correct a chemical imbalance in their brain?

It's frustrating to think we live in the twenty-first century and we are still demonizing people for having mental illness. There is so much paranoia and fear around being labeled "mentally ill" that a lot of people forgo treatment with a medical professional and, instead, seek out ways to self-medicate . . . using alcohol, drugs, food, sex, et cetera to balance out what's happening inside their brain—often to their own detriment.

I believe we, in the United States, are in the middle of a sea change. More people are coming forward to talk about their battles with mental illness; films, television, books, and music are building narrative storylines around mental health issues; there's a thriving online conversation about mental health on social media—and all of this mass-media education is slowly contributing to the dissolution of the stigma around mental health. I hope that in the coming decades the conversation about mental health will become as standard as the conversation around illnesses of the body . . . here's to living in a future world where we embrace our differences (no matter how great or small) and love one another because of those differences, not despite them.

With that said, what I'm *really* here to talk about is my own personal experience with mental illness. Not as the daughter of mental-health-professional parents, but as someone who has found herself lost inside a deep, dark hole without any means of escape. It's a terrible thing to find yourself crying for no discernible reason, to feel utterly alone when you're standing in the middle of a room full of people, to feel like you're living underneath a gray cloud and there's no hope of that cloud ever dissipating. Depression is miserable, and it isolates you in a dark way that makes it really hard for you to find your way back to the light.

As a creative person, I have always felt emotions very strongly—both the good ones and the bad ones. But it wasn't until I went through a really traumatic breakup that I found myself utterly unable to cope. Let's just say that I listened to one particular Death Cab for Cutie album on repeat for about three months straight and sobbed like an idiot over each and every song. My ability to jump-start happiness was offline. I walked around in a fog and cried myself to sleep at night. It was awful and demoralizing.

After months of floating around like a wraith, I was encouraged by my dad and my doctor to try an antidepressant to see if a little chemical rebalancing wouldn't help get me out of the hole I was stuck in. I was lucky, and the antidepressant worked for me. It squeegeed the fog out of my brain, let the light back in, and helped me to see that, though the breakup was tough, I was tougher and would survive it. All I can say is thank God I wasn't so far gone that I couldn't listen to the people around me. If I hadn't been open to their suggestion, I might still be walking around in depression purgatory—and that sends chills of fear down my spine.

Taking something to even out my brain chemically was only the first step. I also immersed myself in therapy. I knew I needed to talk about my feelings and deal with the stuff I'd been bottling up so that I didn't unconsciously find myself repeating bad habits from old relationships in my new ones. I worked with a great therapist for a while, but then my life got crazy and I stopped going regularly . . . and then I stopped going at all.

Not smart, Benson.

As I said in the title of this essay, therapy is the gift I

give myself. It's the safe space where I can go and talk about what's happening inside my brain. It's where I am not alone and where there is always someone thoughtful waiting to listen to me. Someone who will not judge me—even when I'm being a total idiot and making dumb choices—and who will help to guide me back to the path of the (reasonably) straight and narrow once I am in the right headspace to own all of those dumb choices I made and the bad feelings I let overwhelm me.

I am back to seeing a therapist once a week. She is amazing, and I am super lucky to have found her. After my most recent breakup (breakups are a stressor for me), a friend saw I was struggling and recommended I give her therapist a call. I hemmed and hawed—even though I've been to therapy off and on throughout my adult life, it never gets any easier to make myself go back again when I fall off the horse—but, eventually, I stopped dragging my feet, admitted I was drowning, and decided to pick up the phone and ask for help.

I know that, for me, realizing I need help and asking for it are two very different things. I'm pretty good about accepting that I'm having trouble . . . but, dammit, it's really, really hard for me to ask for the help I need. I hate it. It makes me feel weak. Makes me feel like I'm a failure because I can't get my brain back online by myself.

I've spent countless hours suffering on my own with depression when I very easily could've already been talking to someone about fixing the problem. Instead, I've dicked around, trying to solve things alone. I ignore the problem, or pretend I'm "okay," or talk about my feelings with my friends—all in hopes that the darkness will somehow go away on its own. But none of the above is a substitute for talking to someone who is a trained mental health professional. As much as your friends love you and want to be there for you, it's not their job to fix you. Ignoring the problem, or pretending "you've got it under control," will only make things worse. A therapist, psychologist, or psychiatrist knows what they're doing (they went to school for a long time in order to do this), and they know how to help you get back on track.

A friend gave me the Virginia Woolf book *A Room of One's Own*, and, as an artist and woman, I immediately took its themes to heart. Basically, in layman's terms, it says that a woman needs to have both freedom and a safe space in which to create. I believe this is a truth, so far as being an artist is concerned—and I also believe you can take Virginia Woolf's notion of having a "safe space" and apply it to mental health.

Whether we like it or not, the stress of being a human being can be overwhelming, and having a safe space to talk about our problems, assess whether our brains are working correctly, make sure there's nothing chemically out of line . . . well, I think that's super important. I know *I* need that safe space in my life if I'm going to be a productive member of society.

Instead of looking at mental health providers as the enemy, we have to flip the script and look at them as a necessary part of the whole mind/body equation. Did you know that emotional/mental pain lights up the same pain centers in the brain as physical pain? When you think about it, it totally makes sense. So often when I'm emotionally low, my body responds in kind, almost mirroring the emotional distress I'm feeling: I get tired easily; I have full body-and-brain lethargy; I ache all over like I have the flu. It just proves to me that what I'm experiencing mentally is directly tied to my physical health. So by taking care of my mental health, I'm actually also taking care of my body.

And the opposite is true too. I know people with chronic pain, and, invariably, their mental health is compromised by how miserable they are physically.

But what makes things even worse is that we don't exist in a vacuum. We live in a world where we are constantly over-stressed and overstimulated and forced to deal with other people and their needs. You add this "normal" life stress into the equation and everything gets compounded. For me, visiting my therapist is a way to alleviate that stress. If I start talking about all the things that are upsetting me or stressing me out, I find they cease to hold so much sway over my brain. Talking is the way I free myself from all the bad gook and negative thoughts that are getting played on a perpetual loop inside my head.

I'm not saying any of this is easy. It's an uphill battle, and there are lots of setbacks along the way. Like anything, it's a process. One you have to work on consistently. Just finding a good therapist/psychiatrist/social worker/psychologist you jibe with can be a massive pain in the ass . . . and because our health care system treats mental illness like it's not a real disease, taking care of our mental health isn't always covered by insurance—and the financial burden of paying for our own care can be overwhelming.

But there *are* good mental-health-care professionals out there who operate on a sliding scale—which means they will work with you and your income level and make their fees more affordable for you. You just have to start looking for them, and that means asking your support system of friends and/or family for their help. I guarantee you'll be surprised to discover how many people you know who have been in, or are currently in, therapy. They just don't openly talk about it.

Unlike me . . . who wrote an essay about it!

This Is How You Unravel

by E. Kristin Anderson

BEFORE

You bit a nurse.
You won't find this out
until you're in your twenties.

It's a mystery—your memory
seemingly riddled with bullet holes, daily;
some days you wonder what else

you forgot.

***

There are so many blanks
left in the journals.

Like those bullets, or not-bullets—
the ones they use on cop shows
that are empty of ammunition.

The journals are happy
maybe silly—all boys
and friends and wistful
rock-star crushes.

Between the lines is the lie.
Between the lines is your own self
turning against you day by day
by foggy day.

You keep them. This will be your strength.
The words that tangle in your hand
wrap around you like a blanket.

Remember this. Because it starts now.

1.

Eighteen. You've been eighteen
for five months, and May sticks
sticky sweet in the lungs.

87

Remember when you won races?
How that air would rush
into your veins and spin around?
And you'd fall over into the grass
at the finish line. High on this
nerd girl being, finally, a star.

Oh, Poison, she stole that,
didn't she?

***

Shit, it's not really her fault.
She's just one player,
racing shoes and all. But she's
a voice that you could hear,
just a few weeks ago.

A voice with a body attached.
A voice with a face that
you could tell Dr. Whoever about.

Seventeen was better.
Anxious, but proud.
Depressed, but strong.
Seventeen had convictions.
At least Eighteen has him.

***

Red
is a bulldozer.
No.

Red is a butterfly.

Red travels at
the speed of sound
in your brain
the way everything
lights up.

Red is a Christmas tree
and all the presents underneath.

Red is freckles
and the warm
summer sun. He is
raspberry soft serve
and the dark safe
safety.

Red is yours.
You are Red's.
There is nothing else.

***

On your blog
you write about
your life like
it's a movie.

But you've never
been in a movie,
have you?

***

It was March when Poison saw.

You were wearing a pink sweater,
long sleeves, of course.

And she saw. Slick eyeballs
always in the right places.

Or the wrong ones, maybe.

It's not what makes you stop.
But it is what makes it real.

***

You quit with the blade
because you never meant to start.

Okay, sometimes
you use this knife—
a cheap white paring knife
from the kitchen drawer—

but it's too hard. Scratching
the surface is too much,
and you hide the knife
by your clock radio.

But you quit.
You were never good
at it anyway.

***

Last year was a trophy,
ribbons, top seeds, and
cheers in homeroom.

This year you feel the
visceral pang of anxiety
at the track, your home track.

You tell a friend, the one
who competes in your race,
but she's your teammate, too.

Your friend tells you not to race.
She tells you Coach will understand.

The smell of the grass is sharp
like needles, like the sting of
Poison finding a vein.

***

You hear her words and
so viscerally know she's wrong.
But she makes it easy. And easy
is something you can do
when your veins are filled with Sloth.

A deadly sin. That's what she'd tell you
if you'd let her rant about religion.
Funny, that's where you've drawn the line.

Poison is a sinner herself. You know
about her lust. And her lies. You know
about her envy. You know the thin veneer

of innocence that she wears, and you know
that everyone but you believes it.

Still, she says quit. And you absorb
the words like butter in your skin.
And you lie down and close your eyes
and let her win today's race.

***

He picks you up at work.
You're in your red uniform—
no matter, he knows what's
underneath. He says you're pretty.
He gets what it's like to take a pill
and expect sunshine and rainbows
but settle for partly cloudy.

You drive past the mall, hot words
rambling on your warm tongue.
Bands he has to hear and this
one time with Tats, your manager.
You take his hand and he grasps
your fingers and both your hands
cover the stick as you come to a light.

Dairy Queen? he asks.
And you're so for it. He reminds you
of Oz from *Buffy*. Often monosyllabic.
Sincere as hell. Maybe a little werewolf
trapped behind the gate.

You kiss him with sticky
DQ lips and think
> I will marry this boy
> if he'll have me.

***

Yearbooks are out. You go through, page
by page, smelling the fresh ink,
the glossy paper. Look at these photos.
Even you have been caught up in all
the spontaneous camaraderie. As if
the past seven years you spent clawing your way
out of the shadows are as forgotten
as your toddler years. You know they'll
stick to you like hard, chewed-up gum.

There's your page in Senior Superlatives.
Somehow voted Most Unique despite
that one girl who *campaigned* for it.

Mom isn't sure it's a compliment.
It might make you "class freak." You don't care.
You have a title: the Creative One. The One
Who Speaks Her Mind. The One Whose Baby Picture
"Got Lost" Along With Her Senior Quote.

2.

You are eighteen.
Eighteen gives you rights,
you say. Eighteen means
tattoos and cigarettes
and lotto cards.

You only want one
of those things.
And your money is all
tapped out on records.

Your face is hot and wet,
Red is in the kitchen,
your dad stares at you
in your record-store uniform.

Eyes wild. His. Yours too.

He hands over the money,
because you are more terrifying
these days than you are terrified.

***

Windows open,
Route 1 goes to Worcester.
Red's friend in the back.
Alkaline Trio is playing
the Palladium.

Dashboard Confessional is opening.
Boss got you deep-discount tickets,
and it is just so hot.

The AC in Red's car
doesn't work. It's an old Eclipse
with a dent on the hood. He holds
your hand, but you still feel
his friend's eyes. His buddy is older,
thinks he knows everything
about everything.

Maybe it's better
that with the windows down no one
can talk all the way there.

***

At the Palladium
Buddy gets a drink.
You've just changed out of
your work uniform in the lobby
of a bank.

You remember that this morning
you got a tattoo. Red held
your hand while the man
watched *Apollo 13* and
dragged his needle through
your skin.

You keep touching it—
now that the napkin
he taped to you
(is this normal?)
is off, left in a
trash can by that bank.

You touch it
and it feels surreal—
but so does everything
lately—
          unraveling.

***

This morning Tattoo Man
said to Red—not to you—
She's a tough one, isn't she?
He's so impressed
that you didn't cry.
You want to think
you're tough.
You don't know.

Red's friend comes back
with his drink. You hold
on to Red. Together
you're tough. Separated,
you're not so sure.

***

You've stopped watching *Buffy*.

It's not her. She's still
your heart. Your everything
you wish you were. She's still
got Spike hanging around
and a posse of superpowered
cohorts and

there's that new sister.

Maybe it's the villain.

This season seems insurmountable
and so does this day. Today
upon today upon today seems
like a myth.

And the VCR is shit.
You've missed too many episodes.
Good-bye, Buffy. I'll miss you.

***

When you met Red you were
so scared. You knew
that secrets change everything,
that there are people
who think you're just a bitch
or just dramatic or just
one of those acting-out teenagers
from an after-school special.

Sometimes you feel like
Jessie Spano on that
one *Saved by the Bell* episode

where she gets hooked on caffeine.
Except it's not just one episode
and it's not caffeine. It's *you.*

So when you tell Red
in an instant message

>*Hey, I have to tell you something.*
>And he says, *Yeah, okay.*
>And you say *I have depression*
>And he says, *I do too . . .*

well, that's the speed coming down, down, down.

3.

Dad's car is a silver station wagon.
A Ford. It smells stale, like the ghost
of last hockey season. And you sit
in the driver's seat.

You don't remember how you got there.
Dad's cell is in your hands and you dial
one of the only phone numbers you remember:
Grandmother. Grandmother answers and words

spill out of you like a tornado. Trapped.
Scared. Hospital. Liar. Help. Police.

Some part of you knows Grandmother
shouldn't have to feel this feeling.
But the part of you that is screaming,
tearing around your brain like some
lion on fire, it only knows one word:

Escape.

***

Needle. Leather straps. Work clothes stinking
of hospital and tears and sweat.

Black pants black shoes tied with your legs
to the gurney. Lights so bright

your world is a migraine. You are a migraine,
full-bodied delirium, shouting.

Let me go home, you say. *I'm eighteen,*
you say. *Let me go home. I'm fucking fine.*

***

Nimble athlete, bendy thick girl, you
twist and wiggle and wail and finally
find yourself free from the rough
constraint of leather straps.

Nobody is watching. You run.
But you haven't been to this
building before, this hospital
where Mum works. You hate
hospitals. Always have.

Hospitals terrify you. Separate
people into victims and martyrs
and you are neither. And you run,
bare-footed, for where?

There, you see Mum and her friend
in a waiting room, behind glass,
and you run to her feet, hold her leg,
sob into the blue jeans, *Take me home*.
Her friend's eyes are so round, so soft,
so blue. And Mum swells with
unknowing. Mum swells and swells
and swells like a hurricane of
loss and as her eyes go up
a needle sinks into your shoulder.

***

ER Doc ties you back down.
ER Doc makes a deal.
ER Doc uses cloth, lets one arm
be free. Little freedoms. Little
softness. Little little little self
in this prison with no known doors.

***

You ride in the ambulance to Lewiston.
You are eighteen. Your roommate

is elderly. All night, she tells the nurse
that she has to put down her cats.

All night, you replay the way that nurse
checked your body for sharp objects,

handed you the yellow travel bag
from L.L.Bean that your mother packed.

The one you were hoping maybe you'd ask for
for college. With your initials on it.

***

They say that those of us with bipolar disorder
are hard to test. That we manipulate
easily. And that's what you do.

You tell the shrink in Lewiston
that you just wanted your father's attention,
and he sends you home with your mother.

You eat burgers at Roy's. They taste like dirt
to you, still filled with medication. The meds
will sit in your system for days.

And that is your new burden. Pills. More pills.
And you know to take them. You now wear
bipolar like your tattoo. Sort of hidden,

sort of not.

And you will wear it all the way to college
through a summer that exposes you
and the truths of friendships.

Those truths light you up
where the medicine hung like a veil.
And you will take them with you

into nineteen.

4.

You're not the first one
to the dorm; someone
has been there.

Of course it isn't long
before she returns
and the others arrive.

You've brought a whole arsenal
of family—Red included—
where others only have Mom
and Dad.

Red has to leave early.
Mum and Dad have their own
orientation, and then they're gone.

You cry yourself to sleep
on your top bunk, muffling
the sounds with the new pillow
in its new pillowcase.

***

It is October, sweet with fall.
Red hands you the note
with this look on his face
like he just swallowed a brick
or a snake or Jesus.

You unfold the pages, the soft,
simple, lined paper, his somehow
elegant script, so tiny,
resting on the blue and white.
This is not a breakup letter,
it says. That's the opening line.
This is not. But you look up,
and he has tears already
clinging to his eyelashes.

The note is so beautiful.
It's the most beautiful thing
anyone has ever given you.
It's the end. You know it,
even though it says it isn't.

Because you get to the part
where the paper holds these words
to bloom like a climax: *I was*
going to kill myself before I met you.
You made me want to live.

And then, there's this:
I don't know who I am on my own.

Later you'll wonder if anyone else
has kissed their ex good-bye
while they both cried their hearts out.

AFTER

You are thirty. And you don't know the truth.
You are thirty-three. And you don't know the truth.

There are new therapies, new medicines, new ideas,
and while writing, you want to know the truth.
That nurse, the one perhaps bitten—who is she?

Does she bear a scar? Would she hate you? Would she
know you? Is she a she? There is no therapy for lies
passed down to you, through everyone you love,
and you have learned a word: gaslight.

And you are lit up like a candle. You are so lit
and you burn and you won't go out and you hope
that it isn't the gas that fuels you but the whole
of the self that has survived and refused to let go
because of the Reds who have found you.

There are so many Reds in the world.
And there are so many yous.

So far away now, you let the sun hit you in Texas
and know that you have made choices that are
right for yourself, as you wear bipolar
more like a necklace, as you wake in depression
every single day, but you still wake.

And you wake
      and you wake
           and you wake and you put your feet
         on the ground
           and you move.

Some Stuff

by Sarah Fine

I feel like I'm breaking the rules.

I'm about to tell you some stuff, and it's stuff I don't usually talk about. Stuff most people don't know and wouldn't guess. On most days I think I'm in control of it and past it, and on some days I wonder. On no days does this stuff disappear completely, and on all days I use the skills I've learned to manage and master it—even now, when I'm happier in my life than I've ever been.

I'm going to tell you about this stuff because the things that made it hardest for me to get this far might be tripping you up too. Or if not you, then maybe your best friend or your older brother or that girl on student council who seems like she has it all together. I promise you that it's almost impossible to tell sometimes.

Before I get to the *stuff,* though, I'm going to tell you the two reasons why I don't talk about it much. The first: In addition to being an author, I'm a clinical psychologist. A critical part of our training is ethics, including boundaries—how to keep yourself to yourself and only disclose personal information when and if it might actually help your client in reaching therapeutic goals. Disclosure includes what is publicly known, by the way, like what I share on social media or, you know, in anthologies. I've never been much of a rule breaker, but it's not just that. I care deeply about my clients and don't want to do anything that might interfere with or distract from the treatment process.

The second reason I don't talk about this stuff? Well. That's *why* I'm going to talk about it.

There's one experience that I go back to as the moment that divides before and after, even though it's been messier than that. I was sitting in the office of the dorm director. Sophomore year in college. I remember the annoying flicker of the overhead lights and the annoying friendliness on the guy's face. His name was Joel—bland and wholesome and utterly sincere in a way I found totally off-putting, and no more so than this moment when he smiled and told me he'd called this meeting "just to check in."

He asked me how I was doing.

I cheerfully told him I was doing great.

He was quiet for a minute. No idea what was scrolling through his head, but maybe it was the same thought running through mine: *This is a very stupid game.*

We both knew the only reason I was sitting there was

because I wasn't doing well at all. I just didn't know how *much* he knew. And so we stared each other down, smiling as we played our game of psychological chicken, me clenching my teeth, muscles so tight they were trembling, feeling like I was about to shatter into a billion jagged pieces.

Joel blinked first. "Your roommate came to talk to me. She's worried about you."

S**t. She'd threatened to do this.

I was still smiling. Possibly it looked like my teeth were bared. "I'm actually okay. I go to all my classes—you can check. My midterm grades were good."

"She said you've stopped eating. She said you've cut yourself. Can I see your wrists?"

I don't think I've ever hated another person as much as I hated Joel that afternoon. Well, except for my roommate. I'd never felt so betrayed. What the hell did they want from me? I showed up to class and smiled occasionally and pretended to be alive. All I wanted in return was for everyone else to believe the act. No one needed to know that most of the time I was dead, and the rest of the time I was in so much pain that cutting myself felt like validation and relief in one, both affirmation and deserved punishment. But I kept it all covered up! No one was supposed to notice! I mean, I'd been doing it off and on since I was fourteen, and no one had noticed before. In college, though, in a dorm stacked one body on top of another, hiding was a lot harder.

I still hated her for noticing. And I hated him for calling me on it. Mostly, though? I hated myself for being too weak and pathetic to hold it together. I hated that I couldn't feel happy and connected to other people when everyone else made it look easy. I hated this proof that I was a total loser.

Now Joel wanted to see my wrists. My face was so hot. My eyes burned. My fingers clawed at the hem of my long sleeves, holding them tight over what lay beneath. I was so filled up with humiliation that it was choking me. There was no winning. I was fairly sure that if I said, *no, screw you, I'm out of here*, he wouldn't leave me alone. Worse, he might try to physically stop me, and that was something I was willing to do anything to avoid. So I forced myself to let go of my sleeves and turned my palms to the ceiling, defeated. He said I should go to the counseling center.

I told him I wasn't going to go to counseling.

That's when *should* became *would*. Gentle smile in place, he said that if I didn't go voluntarily, "we" would have to consider some other options, like working with my advisor to reduce my course load. Like calling my parents. This a-hole planned to snatch away the one reason I still got out of bed and crush the hearts of the only two people who still believed I was well and whole and worthy.

I told him I would go to counseling.

That afternoon I found myself sitting in the waiting room at the counseling center. Joel walked me down there, explaining that he just needed to stretch his legs and pretending that he wasn't worried I was going to stroll right on by the building unless I had a personal escort. He checked me in. Then, thank the sweet lord, he let the secretary keep an eye on me and left me alone there.

I had always been a good girl. I never got in trouble, ever. I got good grades. I played tennis. I was in the choir. I was the star of the play. I was in too many clubs to name. I worked so damn hard to convince everyone that I was perfect, bullet-proof, headed for great things, well adjusted, excelling.

Now I'd been exposed for the failure I was. Sitting there, out in the open, I wanted so badly to be invisible. I drew my knees against my chest and curled myself as small as I could. Everyone who looked my way could see how sad and broken I was. No one else had ever been this pathetic.

Those lies were pretty deeply embedded. My brain had become my enemy. My shame had kept me from seeking help that I obviously needed. So I still don't know where my next thought came from. It's something of a miracle. And here it is:

Everyone else in this waiting room is here because they need help too.

That was it. Nothing profound. Just a simple, accurate thought.

It was the beginning of after.

After has been a long, bumpy road, and I'm still walking. It has involved seeking treatment (more than once) and learning to accept support from people who care about me. I did not get here by myself, but I have worked hard, and I am proud of that.

For people dealing with mental illness, getting help and

journeying toward recovery involves a number of hurdles, not least of which is stigma. Most of us are aware of public stigma, false and negative beliefs held by other people about what it means to have depression, anxiety, an eating disorder, et cetera. If you don't think you've come across it, ask yourself if you've ever heard someone casually dismiss another person's behavior or personality as "bipolar." Think about how many believe that mental illness equals violent and unpredictable behavior, that depression is a self-indulgent weakness someone can snap out of if they try hard enough, or that anorexia is a condition that could be fixed if that stubborn girl or boy would just *eat something*, for pity's sake. Public stigma is real, even though there are a few indications it's getting better, like surveys that show more people understand the causes of mental illness as neuro-biological (translation: NOT YOUR FAULT) instead of sprouting from flawed character. The same surveys also show many misconceptions persist. Being public about having a mental illness involves the risk of being misjudged. And I think that was part of why I had fought so hard to conceal how much I was struggling. But it wasn't the only reason.

There have been several studies on this thing called *self-stigma*, and some have found that it might be even more important than fear of discrimination in terms of getting help. That's when some of those misconceptions are internalized—they've taken up residence in your head like squatters. They cling like freaking barnacles. They've stitched themselves to your frontal lobes. It's damn hard to kick them out.

Self-stigma is dangerous. It makes a gut-wrenchingly hard thing much harder. You already feel bad, less in control, scared to death, and then you deal with the shame of feeling weak, like a failure. *As a result, you are far less likely to seek the help that could save your life.*

If my roommate (to whom I will always be grateful) had not been willing to risk my friendship for the sake of trying to help me, self-stigma would have continued to hold me hostage. If earnest, sincere Joel (yes, I'm grateful to him, too) hadn't backed me into a corner, and if he hadn't walked me to that waiting room, who knows? It might have won.

There was a recent study that revealed that a significant percentage of medical students—who you'd think would be more informed about mental illness and therefore more likely to recognize it and get help when they need it—are less likely to seek help for depression because it would make them feel *less intelligent.*

The irony is astounding, right? And so painful. So unfair.

But it's part of why I haven't often talked about my own experiences in the past—and it's why I'm talking about it now. If you have ever felt this way, I want you to know that you are far from being the only one.

It's too easy to walk around in pain every day and think you're the one loser in the bunch. It's too easy to look at other people and think that *of course* they are perfectly happy, and they *never* feel like their mind is a feral animal that could turn on them at any moment. It's too easy to let whatever chemicals are bathing your brain in deceptive thoughts (that lead to wild fears that lead to a racing heart and uncontrollable tears and the certainty that you'll never be happy and the urge to disappear forever) also convince you that it's all your fault. It's too easy to wonder why the hell you can't figure it out.

So easy that I still wonder. Yep. I have a PhD in this field. I've got decades of experience, both professional and agonizingly personal. I'm a functioning human, and I haven't hurt myself in over twenty years, even during the most stressful dark times. I know very well that I'm not a loser or a failure. And STILL I fight shame every time I think about telling someone what I've written here.

I'm telling you, though. That is one way you fight self-stigma. It's called strategic self-disclosure. You tell people you think will understand because they have an accurate understanding of mental illness (acknowledging that not everyone does). You also connect. When you're able, as I am now, you advocate for yourself and others.

You learn to be kind to yourself. You learn to talk back to those ridiculous, deceptive, oppressive thoughts. You practice, because goddammit, it takes practice. You listen to what your brain is saying, and you argue when it doesn't make sense.

I do this every single day. It's more automatic now. I pay attention to how I'm feeling, and when my mood changes, I know to follow the thread all the way back to the thought that made the wind shift. I pull that thought out of my brainpan and hold it up to the light.

I'm doing it right now, in fact. Because as I've been writing this, a few thoughts have tried to twist me up:

You don't really understand what you're talking about.

Um, I think I do. Don't make me explain why, brain. You were there.

You're not saying anything people don't already know.

Never hurts to hear the good stuff more than once.

This is gonna be the worst essay in this whole anthology.

LOL. Maybe? I mean, *look* at who else is contributing. It's damn good company. And I was invited to this party.

Next time you interview for a job, what are you going to do if they've read this essay and are concerned that you disclosed too much?

I'm going to smile, and this time I won't be clenching my jaw and baring my teeth. I'm going to explain that I chose to be open and honest instead of buying into self-stigma. I'm no less a professional for having lived through all of it. I'm no less a writer. I'm no less a person. Like everyone else, I'm more than the sum of my experiences—I'm what I made of them. And when I was given the chance to share those experiences with readers who might be looking for connection and validation and hope, I took it.

And it was worth it.

Beyond the Bottom

by Kelly Fiore-Stultz

Rock bottom.

God, I hate that phrase. Mostly I hate it because it gives the illusion—a false claim—of an end point. A place where an addiction cries "uncle" and throws down its weapons.

The truth?

That place doesn't exist. There are no rocks waiting for you. There is no bottom for you to stand upon as you weep or wail.

What *does* exist is an abyss. An abyss you have to travel through, push through, claw through. It's just your choice on how you do that—on what you carry with you, on who you have on your journey, and on how honest you want to be while you do it.

My personal abyss expanded over the course of one decade—from 2000 to 2010. During those ten years, I barely said a handful of words to my younger brother, who was addicted to opioid medications—first Norco, then Percocet, and finally OxyContin. When I did speak to him, I only used all of the worst words a person can say to someone they love.

Or someone they should love, anyway. Used to love.

I think I can say pretty confidently that, during that time, during all ten of those years, I did not love my brother. Or, more accurately, I did not allow myself to love my brother. I was willing to shut off the parts of my heart that remembered our mutual childhood. In fact, I was eager to do it—it was a refuge, that denial. I didn't have to claim my brother and all his failures. I didn't have to own up to what OxyContin was doing to our family.

I spent ten years being hurt instead of being happy, even when my grudges were all that fueled my anger.

Throughout that time I learned that it's pretty easy to tell if someone hasn't dealt with addiction, at least in an up-close and personal way. Upon hearing your story, upon learning of the addict in your life, these people say things to you like "I hope he survives this" or "I hope she gets help" while giving you an encouraging smile or pat on the back. The overwhelming wish from others is that the addict in your life will get better.

What these friends and strangers don't understand is that we—the people who care about this addict, the people who live day in and day out with the ravages of their dependency on substances—don't wish for wellness nearly as much as we wish for an end. Even if that end means death.

When my brother was deepest in his OxyContin addiction,

I wished for his death on a fairly regular basis. I would dream of a world where my parents were not tethered to his needs, where they could travel and not worry about their house being robbed by their own son. I wanted more for them and more for me. I didn't really care what "more" my brother got. He'd already taken so very, very much. So, the truth is this: Death is not the worst outcome when it comes to your addicted relative or friend. Death is a glorious option compared to one more day of this life lived this way.

When my brother first became addicted to OxyContin in the early 2000s, I didn't understand the fundamental truth about opiates—that, after a while, it is no longer about getting "high." It's about staying "well." My brother medicated, then overmedicated, to chase any semblance of a high. But it didn't take long until that high wasn't the goal—the goal became avoiding the debilitating dope sickness that overshadowed and threatened his very consciousness.

Addiction is hard because we perceive it, culturally, as weakness, not as biology. Even lifelong smokers who get cigarette-induced lung cancer aren't treated with the same contempt as addicts are. The closest thing I can find, I think, are the veterans of Vietnam or other wars who flood our homeless populations in our biggest cities. Like addicts, they are looked at as failed versions of humanity. As though their wrongness or badness was only bound to spill out and over. It just took the drug to prove it.

It wasn't until I tried opiates myself that I finally understood. See, when you are addicted to opiates, you are always doing two things at once—chasing something you can barely understand and running as far away from reality as possible.

My own personal foray into using painkillers came the way most people begin using any prescription medication—*with a prescription*. In 2008, when my son was born, he had a traumatic birth. I was prescribed pain pills to deal with the recovery—but, in reality, I ended up relying on the numbing effects of the drug on my fragile psyche. I had a bout of post-partum depression that felt otherworldly. I felt both completely out of control and totally trapped. It was terrifying.

However, when I took painkillers, everything else became . . . tolerable. I learned you could be dependent on something and still function. So I worked every day. I balanced my checkbook. I grocery shopped. I went to parties and concerts and dinners. I socialized with friends and colleagues. I laughed. I cooked. I lived. And I raised my little boy.

And, for nearly a year, I took Vicodin or Percocet to do it.

Since then, what I've come to realize about myself—and, subsequently, about my family tree—is that we have a genetic legacy, fulfilled almost accidentally. When prescribed certain medications, we often become dependent on them to function. It isn't about getting high. It's about staying normal.

My brother's sobriety, and my own, has been vastly successful. This is both in spite of and due to the overprescription of, then complete government crackdown on, opiate pain medications in the US and around the world. When OxyContin became impossible to get locally, my brother was given two doors he could have walked through—one was driving to Baltimore to score heroin, and the other was to enter a Suboxone treatment program. The latter, like the more well-known methadone, is a blocker drug that helps to wean addicts from their opiate. My brother chose the Suboxone program, along with the individual and group therapy that was an essential part of the recovery process. My recovery was slightly less intricate—eventually, I weaned myself down, then off the painkillers that made my life seem so much easier.

But an addiction remains a pervasive sore for a long time. It festers. It erupts. It's like a volcano of hurt that is rumbling just below the surface. Still, in our family, gatherings can be tense. Forgiveness is a very difficult and bitter pill to swallow when you aren't actually feeling all that forgiving.

But it did come back—the forgiveness, the trust.

And especially the love.

I have one memory of my brother that always feels significant, a memory that is somehow metaphoric when you consider all we've been through. When I was eleven or so, my brother and I went fishing during a camping trip with our parents. My dad used to fashion us some poles out of long branches, line, and a hook when we were doing simple dock fishing. I'd slide a kernel of canned corn or a piece of worm on the hook and drop it into the water beneath the dock, waiting for the sunnies to go after it. Sometimes I'd throw my pole back over my shoulder, as though attempting to serve a tennis ball. It was improvised and useless casting, but it made me feel like my line was going farther in the water.

We were standing at the lake's edge one time when I pulled such a move. I threw my arm back and yanked forward, only to feel resistance. A tug. I turned around to see my brother standing behind me, my hook caught on his cheek, just below his eye. He blinked at me a few times, and I dropped my stick, screeching for my dad.

The hook hadn't gone far into his skin, though Dad still needed to pull it out with pliers. My brother, though? He essentially shrugged it off. He let Dad remove the hook, then went back to fishing. He accepted my apology without a second thought. He could have lost his eye. I could have hurt him far worse. But he didn't dwell on that—he just focused on the present. And the present was good. It was worth focusing on.

I've seen my brother in all kinds of situations. High as a kite. Passed out. Bleary-eyed. Angry and dope sick. Handcuffed. Overdosed on the basement floor. I've seen him with the same eyes in all of these ways, and I know one thing for sure—my brother, the addict, is the same boy who went fishing with his big sister. He is the same boy who, for better or worse, can favor being happy over being hurt.

Recovery is messy. It's cumbersome. It's both resilient and impossibly delicate. But there's no bottom. On the contrary, addiction and recovery have one thing in common—they are bottomless. Endless. And one of them is impossibly, indescribably beautiful.

All I See Is Hope

by Ellen Hopkins

I guess I've been blessed with rock-solid genes, at least when it comes to mental health. Despite being bullied relentlessly as a kid and surviving a physically abusive young marriage, I've never suffered from depression or post-traumatic stress disorder, nor considered suicide. At the lowest points in my life, and there have been many, I've always discerned threads of light through the darkness and followed them to the far side.

But I've experienced mental illness through my grandson, Clyde. As chronicled semi-fictionally in my *Crank* trilogy, my daughter (Clyde's mother) has battled meth addiction for more than two decades, cycling in and out of recovery, only to succumb to eventual relapse. In that time, she has given birth to seven children, each with a different father. My husband and I have raised a number of them. We adopted the oldest when he was just a baby. (As I write this, he's almost twenty.) The youngest just turned two and is the only one who lives with my daughter. She had him in jail after yet another backslide.

Her second and third children, both daughters, live with their paternal aunts, one in California and the other in Arizona. They've been there since my daughter's actions sent her to prison in 2002. When she was released two years later, she worked programs (Alcoholics Anonymous and Narcotics Anonymous) for a while, and it was in AA where she met Clyde's father-to-be.

I don't know a lot about the man, who I've met exactly twice, but my daughter did tell me he has a history of mental illness. That, coupled with their falling back into the addictive cycle, fueled Clyde's early childhood trauma. There was likely drug use while he was in utero, and definitely in home after his birth. His parents fought far too often, a serious by-product of the fly-and-crash cycles meth induces.

Eventually they broke up, and I was grateful for that. But then came another man, and another baby, with similar results. The routine was repeated.

I wasn't privy to all the details. My daughter was secretive and manipulative. I only heard from her when she needed something, usually money. But they did visit from time to time, mostly at Christmas, and I sometimes traveled south from my home in Reno to theirs in Las Vegas. I was aware of some problems and sent Child Protective Services in to check on the children on a couple of occasions. CPS would instruct my daughter to keep food in the house and clean the urine-soaked carpets (and kids and Chihuahuas), but never chose to remove the kids. I assumed they were safe, despite the Chihuahuas.

Truthfully, Clyde has never been an easy kid. He's brilliant—his IQ recently tested at 144—and was always determined to know how things work. I remember him as a baby in a walker figuring out the buttons on the TV and remote controls, and as a toddler pulling up chairs so he could reach switches and turn them on and off, seeing which fixtures they operated. He would repeat behaviors (for instance, opening and closing blinds over and over), early signs of the obsessive-compulsive behaviors we see in him today.

He was also prone to tantrums above and beyond the kind most little kids indulge in. If he didn't get his way, he would throw himself on the ground, hard enough to bruise his face and/or for lumps to form on his head. There were times we had to restrain him in our arms for several long minutes to keep him from serious injury. But we always believed it was something he'd outgrow eventually.

I was only peripherally aware, through scattered conversations with my daughter, that once he started school he was confined to special programs designed to limit his more radical behaviors, with the hope that his specialized classrooms would allow him to learn. As far as I know, he was never behind in school, thanks to a true desire to know more about the world he lived in. Math and science have always keenly interested him, though books are his haven.

At home it was rare for him and his siblings to play outside. Rather, they were babysat with screens. The content of the movies they saw and video games they played were legions too mature, and often overtly violent. There was little real oversight, bedtimes fluctuated wildly, and there were days when all they had to eat was ramen. Sometimes they ate it raw. These things we discovered after the children were placed in our care.

It started with yet another new boyfriend, one who brought meth into the house and encouraged my daughter out of sobriety. She'd been clean for a few years, at least to my knowledge. But I started getting calls from her boss that money was disappearing from work and that he thought she might be using. I'll never forget how he finished our final conversation. "I fear for her children's safety."

When a relative stranger declares something like that, your own anxiety level rises. Several phone calls to my daughter made me believe she was, indeed, using again. Worse, she refused to tell me where the kids were. I finally tracked them down in a seedy casino hotel room with the boyfriend's brother, who was fresh out of jail and crashing off Ecstasy. They hadn't seen their mom in close to three weeks and hadn't eaten in two days. Poor Clyde had been trying to steal food so his little brother and sister wouldn't go hungry. All three were in dire need of baths, clean clothes, and a hot meal.

When they recognized me, the children, ages three, four, and nine at that time, ran into my arms. I did what most grandparents would do—put them in a car and drove them

450 miles away from distress, to my stable home. A judge granted us temporary, and then permanent, guardianship. The real journey began.

Talk about lifestyle adjustments, all the way around! For my husband and me, it meant the childless years sliding into retirement were suddenly nowhere in sight. Spare-time pursuits were put on hold, and disposable income shriveled. There were child seats in the cars again, pediatrician appointments for overdue vaccinations, teeth that needed to be filled and capped, orthodontia to consider.

For the kids, the meals we offered were appreciated on one level: We never missed a mealtime. But my household has always enjoyed fresh food, prepared wholesomely, and the kids weren't sold on what I was offering. Vegetables? No way, unless I was counting French fries. Fruit? Nothing but bananas. Meat? Only hamburger would do. Sandwiches? One wanted only peanut butter; the other two wouldn't touch it.

The youngest two children were petrified of being bathed and shampooed, and the three-year-old, who was still in Pull-Ups, screamed at the sight of the toilet. I have no idea what happened to them in the bathroom before they came to us, but it must not have been pretty. As for the bedtime routine, remember, these kids came from a house that often didn't sleep. And neither did they. It took weeks to establish a proper cycle, and that was especially tough for Clyde, who had to be up in the morning to catch the school bus.

When we first took custody, it was October, and Clyde still

hadn't started school. We enrolled him in the fourth grade at the closest elementary, which happens to be relatively small. That was a good thing because he didn't go unnoticed or without offers of help, though at first his teacher enjoyed what therapists call "the honeymoon period," when he managed to keep his emotions in check. But after a while problems surfaced.

There were times when Clyde would retreat into a corner, pull his shirt up over his head, and break down in tears. Other times he'd simply get up out of his seat without permission, go to the office, and demand to speak to his counselor. He had problems controlling his anger and couldn't deal well with other children, so he didn't make friends. He was driven to stay in control and always needed to win at games or sports. If he didn't, he'd melt down completely. And, even at nine years old, he had a mouth that could rival any soldier's, utilizing the f-word (and worse) regularly.

I'd forgotten he'd been in special-ed classrooms in prior years and had no clear idea about the extent of his problems. Eventually, his IEP (Individualized Education Program) followed him from Clark County to his new Washoe County school, and it was then things started to fall into place. Everyone—teachers, principal, counselors, and us parental figures—scrambled to give him the resources he so desperately needed.

If the honeymoon was over at school, things were no better at home. The meltdowns came regularly, over simple requests like doing homework or playing with the dogs. On a few occasions we went out to dinner, and he'd decide there was nothing on the menu he was willing to eat. If we didn't leave, he'd throw screaming fits. A couple of times I had to pick him up off the floor and carry him out the door. Sometimes we had to physically restrain him to keep him from hurting himself or others.

Parenting the standard way didn't work at all. The usual reward and punishment systems meant nothing to Clyde because, after his early childhood experiences, he wouldn't trust our word when it came to promised rewards, and punishments like grounding were laughable to a child who'd suffered far worse in the past. His anger was palpable, and he was pissed at everything—his mother, his siblings, his teachers, my husband, and me. Men especially drew his ire because it had been men who so negatively impacted his formative years.

When his temper erupted, he punched stuff. He slammed, kicked, threw, and broke things. He locked himself in his room or ran away, sometimes staying gone for hours until he cooled off enough to come home. Often he'd freak out over small annoyances like his little brother smacking his lips or chewing with his mouth open. Clyde would yell for the noise to stop, and if that didn't work, he'd lash out.

If we tried to discipline him, he'd shriek and swear, or simply withdraw into some inner place we couldn't reach. After a while, he always surfaced again and acted as if nothing had ever gone wrong. We grew frustrated. Irritated. Sometimes scared—for Clyde, and for the rest of the world with him in it. At one point we considered hospitalization.

But then there were days when none of this happened. Mornings when he'd come into the kitchen, asking to help fix breakfast. Afternoons when he'd play reasonably with his little brother or our new puppy. Evenings when he'd give us hugs for no reason at all, other than he wanted the contact and to let us know he was feeling the love, and when he'd smile, rewarding us with a glimpse of his heart, which is huge and hungry for affection. We could see the child he was meant to be, and that made us more determined to chip through the barriers.

At school, his teachers would glimpse the "other" Clyde too, when he wanted to help out with younger kids or volunteered to clean desks. But inevitably "problem" Clyde would appear, and he'd be sent to the office, where he could work under his principal's supervision. In the quieter setting, he finished his assignments, earning As, but the situation was hardly ideal.

Clyde's counselor wanted to label him ADHD, as too many children are indiscriminately tagged, and medicate his symptoms away. But I saw several things she didn't, including his ability to focus for long periods of time when something interested him. We took him to an amazing psychologist who spent a week testing and observing him. She eschewed the too-easy answers and told us though some of his behaviors seemed on the surface symptomatic of ADHD, what she discovered was PTSD, caused by early childhood trauma.

Clyde had described watching his mother be beaten, as well as her father (my ex), who'd lived with them for a while and served as the kids' protector until the new boyfriend moved in. He told of being pushed outside when he tried to save his mom from injury, and how he'd done his nine-year-old best to break down the door to rescue her and his siblings. He described the pain of his mom making his grandpa move out, rather than her abuser. Of choosing her boyfriend over her children and leaving them alone in a run-down hotel room with a stranger. And these were just the things he could articulate.

We learned about Clyde's brain. His problems stem from damage to the prefrontal cortex (PFC), the part of the brain that regulates behavior, controlling emotions and impulses. This includes making choices between right and wrong, and predicting the likely outcomes of one's actions: *If I choose to do this, this negative result might happen.* It has been called "the seat of good judgment."

The PFC is easily damaged, and trauma is often a factor. Injured pathways between the PFC and the rest of the brain can exacerbate emotional distress or make it difficult to discern appropriate behavior. The prefrontal cortex also helps to focus thoughts, which enables people to pay attention, learn, and concentrate on goals, so impairment can lead to, or be mistaken for, ADHD.

For Clyde, information enters his PFC correctly. But sometimes, depending on his level of stress or if there's excessive stimulation, his "processor" can't handle the input. His thoughts jumble, and he overreacts or underreacts. Often, after an incident, if you ask him why he did what he did, his sincere answer is, "I don't know."

Once we understood the mechanics, it became easier to view his behavior through different lenses. We found a therapist who gave him tools, but who also encouraged us to learn to parent differently. Though it seems counterintuitive, we step away from his meltdowns, rather than wading into them. I'd like to say that we no longer get angry when he curses at us, but that wouldn't be true. What is true is that we now allow him to vent; then once he cools off, we discuss an appropriate consequence. He's beginning to accept them.

School continues to be a challenge, but we've worked with the district to provide Clyde with programs that allow him to interact in general education classrooms, while giving him the ability to retreat into specialized classrooms with excellent support staff available. He's made one really good friend, and that gives us hope that he'll make more, though he's just started middle school, where everything feels confusing. We tell him seventh grade always feels confusing.

As he enters adolescence, things will probably change again. The PFC is the last section of the brain to mature and doesn't develop fully until around age twenty-five. This late growth is a double-edged sword for Clyde, as excessive behaviors are often the hallmark of the teenage years, but there is also the real possibility that he will outgrow many of them.

It's been three years since Clyde came to live with us, and

with lots of help, understanding, and love, he has advanced light-years. The meltdowns, which once occurred several times a day, now happen once or twice a week. They're not as severe and don't last very long. Rarely does he use the f-word or scream at his siblings. He still has problems relinquishing control, and that results in OCD behaviors like needing his toothbrush to be in a certain position in a drawer or wanting to use a specific towel. Small battles we don't need to fight.

Truly, his transformation is amazing, and any time I feel challenged by something he does, I take a deep breath and remember not only how much he's changed, but also how hard he's worked to get better. When he launches one of his less frequent tantrums, I step back to let him vent and cool off. And when he comes to me for that hug that lets him know all is right between us, regardless, I take a very long look at his very big heart.

And all I see is hope.

PS: Just as I was thinking this story was finished, with a killer last line, I wandered down to the family room, where the kids were staring at the TV. I asked what they were watching, not so much because I was worried about content, but rather simply to make conversation. Instantly Clyde flipped the channel. "I was just changing it," he swore.

The other kids rolled their eyes.

This *Thing* Inside Me

by Scott Neumyer

I have a confession to make. I've lied. A lot.

No, not big, life-altering lies. I've never cheated on my wife or broken the law or been unethical in any way in any of my careers. I've played all those games by the book.

But over the past decade or so I've told more lies than I can even count. Some of them I probably don't even remember telling. Some of them I've probably convinced myself at this point that they *weren't* lies. That the things I said and did were, in fact, the truth.

I'm too smart, however, to think (even for a moment) that I've been completely honest with myself and everyone around me for quite some time.

So now you know. I'm a liar. A big, filthy, stinking liar.

But wait! Before you flip the page and move on to someone else's story, thinking that they're more genuine and heartfelt and moving than me, stick around for a few minutes and keep reading.

I'm a good guy. I really am. I promise. I may have lied countless times over the past ten or so years, but I'm really a good, nice, smart guy. Seriously! Just ask my mom!

You see, I've never really *wanted* to tell lies. I've always prided myself on being honest and shooting straight with people. You need someone to tell it like it is? I'm your guy!

But when it comes to *me*, that's where the trouble begins, because I have this *thing* inside me—this weird little voice— that's always telling me what to do, and I'll be damned if I can get it to shut up.

Okay, before I get all Jiminy Cricket on you or finally tell you about some of the crazy things I've lied about, let me go back to the beginning. Let me take you to the moment this *thing* started to creep up inside me like the chest burster in *Alien*.

I'm thirty-six years old now (I know . . . I know . . . I'm old!), so I was maybe twenty-four when it all started.

My girlfriend at the time (now my wife and the mother of my children) decided to take me into New York City to see *Rent* for my birthday. We'd known each other since high school but only started dating about five months prior to the trip, and it was our first birthday celebration together.

Early that morning we got a ride into New Brunswick, New Jersey, and hopped on a train bound for the Big Apple, a trip we'd both taken many times before.

With plenty of time to spare once we hit Manhattan, we

decided to grab dinner before heading over to Broadway. And that's when the trouble started.

We weren't two bites into our meal when Denise excused herself to the bathroom. She seemed worried, but I waited as she ran off. It was about five minutes before she returned in a rush.

"We have to go," Denise said. "We have to go now. Right now."

I couldn't tell if she'd been crying or if there were beads of sweat running down her cheeks, but I could tell instantly from the look on her face that it was, indeed, time to go.

"Are you okay?" I asked. "Is everything okay?"

"We just have to go. Please. Now. I don't feel well."

And, with that, I grabbed our waiter, paid the bill, and ran outside to meet her, thrusting my hand up to hail a taxi as I stepped onto the sidewalk.

"No cab," she said. "We have to go. Let's just walk fast."

So we speed-walked all the way back to Penn Station, where we were lucky enough to make it just in time to catch the next train back to Jersey.

Confused and worried about Denise, I tried to rub her back on the way home, but the mere thought of being touched at that moment only made her worse. So, instead, I called my parents to pick us up at the station. She played Snake on her Nokia candy-bar cell phone to try to take her mind off whatever was bothering her.

The next morning Denise would head to her doctor,

explain exactly what had happened, and be handed a diagnosis of panic and anxiety disorder.

For the next eight months I watched my girlfriend go through hell while wrestling with her anxious mind as she tried to work, finish nursing school, and be the same social, fun-loving woman she'd always been. I held her hand and rubbed her back and cried along with her when it got harder than usual.

And then, one day, like that familiar scent you can always smell right after the rain stops, it was over. She'd done the work by seeing her therapist, practiced her exposure therapy, and overcome her fears. All without medication.

Yes, she would still have to deal with anxiety from time to time (we all do), but she was no longer afraid of being afraid. She didn't imagine that bear behind the door ready to jump out at any moment. She was *free*.

And that's when I went to see Bruce Springsteen live at Lincoln Financial Field in Philadelphia, Pennsylvania.

I've told this in all its gory detail before in a story I wrote for SBNation.com called "I Am Royce White," but I'll give you the broad strokes:

High up in those bleachers, I alternated between watching the Boss belt out "Thunder Road" and sticking my head between my knees in a *very* public bathroom.

I was miserable and sick and afraid of . . . I had no idea what.

"I think I'm having a panic attack," I told Denise from

inside the bathroom stall. "I can't stop sweating, and all I can think is *RUN NOW GET OUT OF HERE GET HOME.*"

I was sweating so badly that my orange Nokia nearly slipped out of my hands to the floor.

You know that hell I watched my girlfriend go through for eight months? I was in that very same hell. I just happened to be in another state, in a dirty bathroom, with about fifty drunk Springsteen fans wondering when my stall door would open up.

That night was the start of everything for me. It didn't *really* hit me full blast until a few months later when summer was over and I had a major panic attack while substitute teaching a junior phys ed class.

As soon as the bell rang for the end of that period, I told the main office I had to leave and bolted down the hallway to the parking lot, never to teach again.

After about a month of barely leaving my bedroom, let alone my house, I found another job and, bolstered by a whole lot of Zoloft (after watching how difficult it was for my girlfriend to tackle this problem *without* medication, I sure as hell went right for it), started to piece my life back together.

That was over *ten* years ago. A decade, folks. Ten long, painful, exhausting, anxiety-filled years.

But guess what? I'm still here.

Now back to where we started—me being a stinking, no-good liar.

So, yeah, over the past decade I've told a lot of little white lies to make myself more comfortable. I mostly told them to get out of doing something or going somewhere that I was sick-to-my-stomach anxious about going.

In those ten years I've lied to my wife and kid about having to work so I didn't have to go on vacation. I've lied about being too busy to watch football with my buddies because I was *scared to watch football with my buddies*. I've faked headaches and backaches and every other kind of ache you can think of to keep me anxiety free in my safe place.

I've lied about eating too much food and about eating too little. I've lied about just about everything to make myself feel better—to not feel the constant pang of anxiety in my gut.

I've lost friends and confounded family, who just can't grasp what's going on inside my mind. I've made myself so sick with anxiety that I basically ruined one of my best friend's wedding pictures.

I've backed out of so many things that even I wasn't surprised at all when my lifelong best friend didn't ask me to be in his wedding. Of course I was bummed about it, but I understood completely. Sometimes I'm surprised I made it through my *own* wedding.

And, I've never admitted this to *anyone* before (not even my therapist), but I've actually thrown myself down a flight of stairs to try to get out of going to a family member's big birthday bash.

What can I say? I feel absolutely terrible about these things I've done. I don't *like* that I lied so much. I *hate* that I backed out of doing things I'll never get to do again (especially when it comes to doing things with my kids). I loathe the fact that I'm the guy who people don't ask to do things because they know I'll just say no now (hey, at least I've stopped lying!).

But guess what? *I'm still here.*

And that's why I've spent all this time talking about all the terrible, stupid, selfish things I've done to quiet that *thing* inside me. I've laid it all out here because I'm tired of lying. I'm tired of backing out. And I'm tired of being "that guy."

And I've also bared the deepest, darkest places in my soul here because I know that *you've* lied too. *You've* backed out. And *you've* been that guy (or girl).

And I'm here to tell you that *it gets better*. It may not seem like it. It may feel like you're Artax from *The Neverending Story*, and you're drowning in the Swamps of Sadness. It may feel too hard. Trust me, I've been there and felt that.

But guess what? *You're still here too.*

And that's the moral of my story, kids. Anxiety sucks with a capital S, but it *does* get better with time, hard work, and help. It truly does.

Ten years ago I was lost and scared and unemployed after running away from the job I had.

Today I'm incredibly proud to be able to say that I've written for publications like the *New York Times*, *GQ*, *Esquire*, *Sports Illustrated*, and *ESPN*. I've held long-term jobs, become an editor, and won an award for telling my story. And I've been able to write about mental health awareness and breaking the stigma of mental illness in this country time and time again.

I have a wife and two amazing kids and a couple of cats, all living under the same roof.

I still have rough days and plenty of times when my anxiety gets the best of me, but I've learned to tell that *thing* inside me to shut up and leave me alone for a while.

This, folks, is what you can look forward to if you keep your head up, ask for help, and do the work.

Anxiety feels like you're falling into a dark pit, and you just keep falling and falling and falling. But, trust me when I tell you, there's a bouncy house at the bottom, so you're going to be just fine.

For years now I've been saying in my head over and over again that I hope my seven-year-old daughter doesn't turn out like me. Even tonight, as I was rocking my three-month-old daughter to sleep, I actually whispered to her, "Don't be like Daddy when you grow up."

But you know what? Maybe being like Daddy wouldn't be so bad after all.

OCD:
My Tentacled Monster

by Crissa-Jean Chappell

My monster is a sea creature, the kind that crushes your bones to dust. He's curled under my desk right now, listening as I type. He might hook a tentacle around my foot. Tug me underwater so fast I won't see it coming.

He won't let go.

The wall outside Mrs. Kenny's classroom is made of coral rocks. At recess I squeeze my finger into the shell-shaped dents. I start at the top, counting *one, two, three* as I work my way down. Then I do it all over again.

Why am I counting rocks?

Because that's what the monster told me to do.

Today the magic number is three. Tomorrow it's twenty. Odd numbers are bad (except for lucky number three). Even numbers are good. My monster makes up the rules, but for some reason, the rules keep changing.

The other kids have their own rules. Jump-rope rhymes. Hand-clapping chants. Their singsongy games rub against my skin like sandpaper. I drift under a tree with my crayons and doodle stories about the monster inside my head.

Everybody stares.

"What's wrong with her?"

Something is wrong.

If I don't follow the rules, bad things will happen. Mom and Dad will die in a plane crash. Our house will burst into flames. My dog, Holly, will get hit by a car.

I have to keep everybody safe.

Mom files her nails as we watch TV. The *scritch scritch* of her emery board makes me cringe. She does this thing—flicking once, twice, three times in a row. Minutes later she does it again.

There's a question floating in my mind.

I'm scared to say it out loud.

"Do you ever feel like . . ."

She looks at me. "Feel like what?"

I feel like I have to do things.

When I walk past the tall, wooden posts in the living room, I feel like I have to touch them. I turn off the light in my bedroom, then I turn it back on. *One, two, three.* I always step into the kitchen with my right foot first. Never the left. Everything has a "right" and "wrong" side.

Mom doesn't say anything. She flicks her nails. "You can make it stop."

Practice.

That's what she tells me.

So I try really hard.

No more turning the light off three times.

Now it's ten.

In high school I spend a lot of time hiding in the bathroom—the safest place I can find during those long, gray days. All the color has drained out of the world. Sometimes I can't stop crying. I don't even know why.

The monster whispers in my ear. It's worse when I'm in class, trapped at my desk. I can deal with his monster babble for a little while. Then I sneak off to the bathroom. The monster says I'll probably fail all my classes. Maybe I'll end up homeless in a cardboard box.

I know these panicky thoughts are garbage.

It doesn't stop me from obsessing.

At night I stay awake for hours, worrying about all kinds of stuff. I try to gulp a breath, but I'm dying in slow motion. That's what it feels like. My heart slams against my ribs. I start counting the spaces between the beats. *One, two, three.* What if my heart stopped beating?

Yeah, I'm a little obsessive.

When people talk about OCD, it sounds like the punch line to a joke. *Oh, I always match my socks and T-shirts. I'm so obsessive-compulsive.*

OCD isn't about matching socks.

It's about a monster squeezing his tentacles around my brain.
Of course, nobody's told me that I have OCD.
I already know.

The summer before my senior year, I'm in the checkout line with Mom at the BX in Homestead (the air force discount store).

"Did you hear about the hurricane?" asks the lady behind us.

I glance at her shopping cart.

It's filled with stacks of batteries.

A couple of nights later I'm crouched in the hallway with my parents and Aunt Frannie. The cats are in the closet. My grandmother's in the bathtub, clutching her rosary. It's so dark, I can't see anything. All I hear is Hurricane Andrew's freight-train howl. Trees thudding against the house. Glass exploding all around us.

I drop my head between my knees and try to block out the noise. For some reason I start counting inside my head. All the people I've ever met. Every movie I've watched. The paperbacks on my shelf, their spines sealed with Scotch tape.

I count for hours and hours in the darkness. The next morning, my books are gone. Now the walls are crusted with seaweed. The pages of my novels-in-progress are soaked. It's only "stuff," but it's my stuff. Our house looks like somebody flipped it upside down and shook it.

We won't have running water or electricity for months.

School—the place I've always dreaded—is the only normal thing in my life. The rest of the year passes in a blur. I help my family rebuild our house. Instead of going away to college, I take classes at the University of Miami. Everything is different and the same.

I want to talk to somebody about the monster.

I mean, really talk.

One day I walk over to the counseling center on campus. My hands won't stop shaking as I fill in the bubbles on a questionnaire. How often do I find myself "feeling down"? Does it ever seem like "anxiety" is getting in my way?

The psychiatrist asks a lot of questions too. She talks about "clinical depression" and "OCD" and gives me a prescription for Paxil. Now the monster has a name—obsessive-compulsive disorder.

"It's just the way my brain works," I try to explain.

At first this Paxil stuff is okay. The monster slowly backs off. I'm floating above the earth, watching everything from a distance. I'm numb, but not so anxious. Then I start to get the "brain zaps." Sudden thunderbolt headaches. Technicolor nightmares. A stomachache that won't go away. I can't concentrate on school because I feel sick all the time.

I dump the bottle of pills in the trash.

The monster is still with me today. When his tentacles begin to squeeze, I've learned to channel my obsessive energy into something more constructive than flicking a light switch. Instead, I'll grab my pens and sketch for hours.

Paxil didn't work out for me, but that doesn't mean I'm against medication. For once, I was finally able to see the world without my "depression goggles." It reminded me of the first time I wore glasses and discovered how foggy my vision had been for years. I had just never realized it.

During therapy I learned something else as well. For the longest time I believed in the myth of the tortured artist, but it's difficult (if not impossible) to create if you're trapped inside a black hole of depression.

I used to believe that antidepressants would drain away my ability to write. To my surprise, I wrote constantly. I filled pages and pages in my journals. A lot of my experiences became the threads of my first published novel, *Total Constant Order*.

Sometimes it takes days to write a single page. I'm so impressed by authors who can crank out a book in a couple of months. I might spend a year working on a first draft, but that's fine. When I'm typing a scene or doodling with a pen, all the static inside my head fades away.

I still struggle with anxiety and depression, but I've made peace with my monster.

When his tentacles begin to squeeze, I'll squeeze back. Instead of pushing him away, we sort of float together, as if we're dancing underwater. All this time I never knew his secret. My obsessive brain isn't a tentacled monster after all.

It's my superpower.

Dirk

by Francesca Lia Block

My friend Dirk and I are drunk in a club, but it's not the usual type of place we hang out. Instead of a dark, dank basement full of punk rockers, this is a chic West Hollywood dance club, mirrored, brightly lit, and full of pretty people in eighties pastel and neon colors. With Dirk's Mohawk and my torn black taffeta 1950s prom dress and steel-toed engineer boots, we really don't belong.

"Here," he says. "Open your purse."

I always do everything he says, like I'm under a spell. I unsnap the clasp on my grandmother's vintage evening bag, and he puts something inside it.

"What was that?" I ask.

"A microphone," he says. "It's really cool-looking. See?" He tugs my purse open a little to show me.

"Is that a good idea?"

"It's fine. Don't worry."

"Okay," I say, not really thinking. I'm just here to hang out with Dirk. I follow him everywhere.

A short time later the loud music comes to an abrupt halt, and a voice comes over the PA system. "It's been brought to our attention that a piece of equipment has been stolen. No one is going to leave until it's found. Please be prepared to have your persons searched."

I turn to Dirk, aghast. His expression hasn't changed.

"Go into the ladies' room," he says, always ready with a solution. "Leave it on top of the toilet in the stall."

I trot off to do as he tells me. My purse is heavy with the weight of what Dirk and I have done. I put the huge silver, phallic-looking microphone on the toilet and hurry back to my friend, the one I look up to, the one who gets me into trouble, the one who scares me sometimes, the one I love.

The one with manic depression, but I won't know this for almost forty more years, and by then it will be too late.

Dirk was a tall, skinny boy with big glasses and acne. Then he transformed into a tall, skinny, tan, preppy boy with green contact lenses who won "best dressed" in the junior high yearbook. Finally, he became a tall, muscular, tan punk rocker with a Mohawk. His clothing choices during this phase were as meticulous as his preppy wardrobe, though now he wore a leather motorcycle jacket, bondage pants, kilts, combat boots, and thick rubber-soled brothel creepers, all purchased from stores on Melrose or thrift shops in the remote reaches of Glendale and the San Fernando Valley.

Dirk and I went to our first punk show together—the Weirdos at the Whisky a Go Go. We'd been listening to punk on Rodney on the Roq's radio show and at Phases, a new-wave disco in the Valley where we went each week, but we'd never been exposed to the music live. Dirk picked me up in his red-and-white 1955 Pontiac convertible, and we rode over Laurel Canyon to the club. His height and imposing hair made me feel safe anywhere. As did the expensive Chablis he'd stolen from his mother's wine cellar earlier that evening.

The music we heard was just what we needed—an embodiment of the frustration and anger neither of us quite knew how to express.

For the rest of that summer before college, we shopped for punk finery, depleted Dirk's mother's wine supply, drove around the city in the Pontiac, and slammed in the mosh pit to punk bands. Late at night we'd get the Oki-Dog: a pastrami, hot dog, and bean-and-cheese burrito, which I ate, even though they made me sick, because Dirk told me to.

Once we ran into a boy we knew from the Valley new-wave club at a punk gig. He was blond and blue-eyed with smooth, white skin and a snub nose. As Aryan as could be, down to the swastika on his sleeve.

"You should go talk to him," Dirk said. "Tell him we can give him a ride home."

I trotted over.

Somehow the boy and I ended up sleeping together on Dirk's bedroom floor. I could tell he was watching us. In the morning, when we got up, one of Dirk's beautiful younger sisters was playing classical piano; the other was making pancakes, and the air smelled of butter and sugar. The punk boy listened to the music, ate the pancakes, then rubbed his eyes as if in disbelief before he put on his army jacket with the swastika and took the bus home.

I went into the bathroom and vomited up my breakfast.

In September, Dirk went off to UC Santa Barbara and I to Berkeley. He visited me a few times, and we saw hard-core punk bands like the Dead Kennedys at the Mabuhay in San Francisco. Our drink of choice was now Bacardí rum that Dirk shared with me from a flask he carried.

Once, in the middle of the night, soon after he'd left Berkeley, I got a call. Music blared; he whispered hoarsely, and I could tell he was drunk.

"What's wrong?"

"I got beat up," he said.

"What? Are you okay? Where are you?"

"I'm at the club."

"You have to get to a hospital." But he told me he was going to go home. "We can't do this anymore," I said.

That was the end of the punk scene for both of us.

After freshman year we ended up back in Los Angeles, sharing a Wilshire-district apartment that Dirk decorated in pale-pink and charcoal-gray mid-century modern. Framed photos of Marilyn Monroe and James Dean hung on the walls. This was the beginning of our rockabilly phase. He sported a black pompadour, and I bought crinolines for our swing-dancing sessions at Club Lingerie and Cathay de Grande. We drove to Orange County to see James Intveld and bands like the Rockin' Rebels and the Red Devils, fronted by a beautiful, pale, sweet-voiced girl with sharp dark eyebrows and perfect cowboy boots. Dirk grabbed me a little roughly and pulled me onto the floor. He'd get a glassy, faraway look in his eyes and sing along, and there was no way you could reach him in that state.

One night we were in our apartment; it was late, after a gig, and hot. He wasn't wearing a shirt. He took me in his arms against his sweating chest and began to dance with me. "I love you," he said. "But we're never going to sleep together."

"I know," I said. At that time I just hoped he'd keep telling me what to do forever, no matter how crazy it seemed.

Dirk became the protagonist in a series of books I wrote and published between 1989 and 2009. I received hundreds of letters and messages from gay boys thanking me for giving him to them. The real Dirk never really liked to talk about his role in my books; I guess it made him feel self-conscious, but it was the best way I knew how to express my love.

Dirk was there through my breakups with various boy-friends, none of whom he approved of. In all the pictures he's smirking snidely at whichever guy happens to have his arm around me. And all of them except Dirk were gone by the time my dad died of cancer. Dirk drove up north to attend my graduation and help me move back to LA.

Later, Dirk became a successful real estate agent, and he and his boyfriend bought, refurbished, and sold a number of stunning homes. They were both at my wedding, two tall, handsome men, perfectly groomed, with matching haircuts, and wearing designer suits.

When I had my children, Dirk and I lost touch. Then, a few years ago, he called. He had left his boyfriend and was living in an expensive hotel in Hollywood, driving a Porsche, and dressing in an even more extravagant style.

"I have all these glamorous friends. We party every night. I hardly need to sleep. It's amazing."

"Are you okay?"

"I'm great! I'm the best I've ever been. How are you and the kids?"

I told him about my housing situation; I'd gotten stuck in the crisis of the early 2000s but had finally convinced the bank to modify my loan.

"You should never have bought that house," Dirk said, the pitch of his voice escalating. "You need to sell it now."

"But I've got it taken care of."

"No, that's a terrible idea. You need to sell it. I'll sell it, and we'll find you a condo."

I didn't want him to tell me what to do anymore. I loved my home; I'd made things work. "It's okay now."

He began screaming at me. I hung up. We didn't speak again.

*   *   *

A few months ago I got an e-mail from Dirk with pictures attached. In the images he looks fit and meticulous as always, dressed in expensive, stylish clothes—bright shirts to show off his tan, perfect jeans, black leather Converse. He poses with young boys, porn stars, and Jack Russell puppies.

Lots of exciting things happening. I need to fill you in. You should come by for a party tonight! he wrote.

Remembering how he'd shouted at me, I only wrote back, *You look great! Hope all is well. xoxox*

A few weeks later one of his sisters left me a message. *Please call me. I need to talk to you about Dirk,* was all it said.

When I called, her voice was high and light, almost giddy. After we exchanged some pleasantries, I said, "What is it?"

"Dirk died," she told me.

He had been living in that hotel room when the depression hit. That was when it became clear that the other behavior— the breakup, the move, the spending, the fights with his family and friends—was the result of mania. The depression was so bad he didn't leave his bed for almost a year. His boyfriend took him in, got him on meds, nursed him to health. When the mania hit again, Dirk stopped taking his meds and moved back to the hotel. The boyfriend had been monitoring his credit card statements and saw that there hadn't been any activity for a few days, so he had the hotel check his rooms. Dirk was found facedown on the bed. His little Jack Russell terrier had been in there with him for days.

I never knew Dirk had been diagnosed with manic depression. I never paid attention to the signs. I let my own dependency issues get me into dangerous situations, which I must have unconsciously blamed him for, so that when he finally turned on me, I had little patience left. He was reaching out to me at the end, and I didn't know how to respond, what to say. In one of the photos he sent, we're in our early twenties. He's got a pompadour, and he's holding me in his arms so that my legs, clad in lace stockings, drape over his arm. His eyes—they look so bright.

Waiting for the Bad

by Tara Kelly

It starts with a thought, a nagging concern. It grows inside my head, taking up more space, slowly suffocating me. Then comes the lump in my throat, the heaviness in my stomach. My heart begins to pound, and my skin hums. I lose control of my breathing. Voices ask what's wrong; they tell me to calm down . . . it's going to be okay. But they're just adding to the distortion in my head. I'm here, but I'm not. I'm waiting for the world to go dark, for my heart to stop. But it just pounds harder and faster until I'm sure it's going to explode. I'm like a car without brakes or a steering wheel. All I can do is keep running. . . .

A doctor once told me I had the worst case of anxiety he'd ever seen. It made me feel even worse, but it probably wasn't an exaggeration. When it gets bad enough, anxiety shuts down my entire life. The worry consumes me. The worst *is* going to happen, and all I can do is wait and obsess. I stop sleeping.

I stop eating. I can't work . . . I can't even leave the house. Nobody—even those closest to me—can convince me it's going to be okay.

Anxiety isn't my only mental "issue" (I also have ADHD and OCD), but it is—by far—the most debilitating for me. After a bad spell, I'm left with nothing but shame and lost time.

Anxiety and mental illness run in my family, and I grew up in an unpredictable household. My mother has Bipolar I, the most severe form, and would experience mania. I remember the panic attacks I'd have every time she didn't come home when I expected her. I was sure the worst had happened, that she'd driven off a cliff or gotten into a horrible wreck. But, luckily for me, she always came home.

A psychiatrist once told me, and studies have also suggested, that childhood trauma like I experienced can rewire the brain, leading to mental illness. I'm no expert, but my theory is that we're born with a susceptibility and our environment can bring it out and make it worse. Even if my childhood had been blissful, I think I'd be a worrywart—it just comes so naturally to me. But I believe the trauma I experienced growing up led to life-altering anxiety.

While I'm speaking to everyone who has anxiety—sometimes you just need to feel like someone out there gets it. I can only speak for myself, but I feel like "waiting for the bad" is my default mode. When things are going right, I'm always looking over my shoulder, asking myself, *What's the catch? When is it all going to come crumbling down around me?*

I work every day to change my thinking—to live in the now instead of worrying about what I can't control. I'm very lucky in some ways. I didn't turn to drugs to cope, like many of my friends did, or end up in jail or on the streets. I used art—my insatiable curiosity about the world around me, about people and why they behave the way they do—as my escape. I'm a fighter. Even when I get knocked down and it takes me months to recover, I *always* get back up.

How Anxiety Took Me Down

My anxiety has always been a hum in the background, something I'm constantly fighting to overcome. I've lost friendships over it. We'd go to a concert we'd been looking forward to for months, and I'd beg to leave because my fear of crowds became overwhelming and I couldn't hold back the panic. In hindsight, I realize they weren't very good friends, but at the time I was furious with myself. I thought I was selfish and weak. I believed people when they said, "You just need to grow a pair. It's all in your head—you *can* control it."

But the more I tried to hide it, the worse it got.

There were two times in my life when it completely debilitated me—I guess you could call them full-on breakdowns. I was twenty the first time, right in the middle of college. I began experiencing symptoms I couldn't explain. Body aches, stomach problems, electrical shocks running under my skin.

I became convinced that my impacted wisdom teeth were infected and the infection was spreading throughout my body. And when that wasn't the cause, I became convinced I had cancer or some mystery disease the doctors had missed. I stopped eating and sleeping—in fact, I went for almost two months eating nothing but a handful of crackers each day. My symptoms—naturally—got worse. One day in class I felt a massive panic attack coming on. I drove myself to the ER, where they had to give me injections of Ativan. And even then my heart rate remained elevated. I'd lost over twenty pounds, and my potassium was through the floor. Oddly enough, I could've died. . . . Not from this mystery disease, but from my own fear.

Anxiety *can* cause harm—it must be taken seriously.

My second big attack came after I got my first migraine with aura. Like my mom, I have complicated migraines that can cause all kinds of fun neurological symptoms—visual disturbances (auras), which aren't much different from an acid trip; hearing loss; dizziness; numbness in the extremities. In short? Sometimes it's hard to know the difference between a migraine attack and a stroke. So imagine what those symptoms do to an anxious hypochondriac. Now add in the fact that my mom has a congenital condition called fibromuscular dysplasia (FMD), which causes narrowing in the arteries and makes a person susceptible to aneurisms and strokes. Her carotid artery dissected when she was thirty-seven—something she thankfully survived. As her daughter (it is far more common in females),

I have a 50 percent chance of inheriting it. You probably see where this is going: Migraines can be triggered and made worse by—you guessed it—stress and anxiety.

This fear didn't take me a couple of months to get over. It took me years—and, truthfully, I'm still not fully over it. Every new migraine symptom brought on a panic attack. It was my worst nightmare, really. Complete lack of control and never knowing what the next migraine would bring. Would my hands go numb? Would I pass out? Would I lose my vision again? Would I be unable to speak? Or was it even migraines at all. . . . Each time I was sure *this was it*—I had FMD like my mom. I was having a stroke. Nothing, not even multiple MRIs and visits to neurologists, could convince me otherwise.

This time it wasn't just *my* life that was impacted—it was my husband's. I'd call him at work, in full panic mode, sure I was having a stroke, and he'd leave in a rush. This didn't happen once—it happened several times over the course of a few months. Sometimes I was so convinced I was dying that I'd say my good-byes to him. And I knew what it was doing to him—I could see the frustration on his face when *nothing* he said worked. I'd gone through it with my mom. The feeling of helplessness. The stress of neglecting your own responsibilities to take care of someone else. The worst part of anxiety, for me, is what I put my loved ones through.

After doing research, I became convinced that the altitude of Colorado was making my migraine attacks worse. No doctor told me this outright. All they said was it's *possible*. But that was all I needed. Something I could control. I could move away. So we did. We completely uprooted our lives, after only six months in Colorado, and moved to Oregon (sea level) where everything was going to be "better," even though we went there with no jobs and no place to live.

But it didn't get better. At least . . . not for a while. Not until I began to understand the power of anxiety, the power of my own mind. If I wanted to get better, I needed to stop running away, face my anxiety head-on, and figure out what worked for *me*.

So, What Works?

Okay, disclaimer time. What works for me may not work for you. We all experience anxiety differently—and we all have different fears. But, hopefully, something here will speak to or inspire *you*.

Medication

This is usually the first thing you'll hear if you go to the doctor, and it does work for some people. But the truth? I don't like medication. I've had too many negative experiences with it (granted I've been put on nearly every "brain-fixing" drug imaginable), and these days I don't take anything because I've gotten better at managing my anxiety. However, in my case, benzos (benzodiazepines) *were* the only thing that stopped my panic attacks. In the past, I'd get a prescription of Ativan from my doctor just *in case* of a panic attack. Knowing it was there, if all else failed, actually helped. You know, kind of like the comfort of knowing you have an emergency brake . . . if you're the type of person who regularly worries about your brakes going out.

Daily Exercise

I can't stress enough how much regular, heart-pounding cardio has helped me. I like to think of it as kicking the hell out of my panic. Going on long walks or hikes in the mountains is especially healing for me. The quiet and the smells of nature give me a sense of calm I just can't achieve any other way. An added perk? I now get a cold—maybe—once every few years.

Getting Outside

If I feel a panic attack coming on, I immediately go outside and start walking. If I can't walk, I just stand and take deep breaths. Don't ask me why this works—I actually have no clue. I think it gives me a sense of escape or the option to run if I need to. For me, closed, tight spaces make my panic/anxiety worse, and open spaces are calming because they make me feel safe. That's the key—finding the one thing that makes you feel safe.

Yoga/Stretching

While I know yoga can fall under exercise—it's not about exercise for me. It's the sense of calm and release I get from stretching and focusing on my breathing. This is particularly helpful when I'm having anxious thoughts at night—it almost always puts me right to sleep.

Keeping a Regular Sleep Schedule

This one is hard for me. I'm an artist! Being unpredictable and spontaneous and staying up until four a.m. writing a song or a book is just who I am. But . . . a regular sleeping schedule is essential for me to help control both my migraines and my anxiety. Since I have a full-time day job, this means going to bed by midnight (okay—by one a.m.) and getting up at the same time each morning. If I'm not strict about this, I get insomnia, and insomnia leads to panic—not fun.

Changing My Diet

I've found eating fresh, unprocessed foods (although sometimes frozen meals are unavoidable due to my work schedule) helps my migraine symptoms. And, in my case, the better I feel physically, the less anxious I feel.

Music/Photography/Art

When you have anxiety like I do, distractions are your best friend. Nothing distracts me better than jamming on my guitar, writing a song on the piano, or belting my heart out to a song. I start playing, and I get lost . . . any worry I have fades into the background. The same goes for photography. I love driving out into the middle of nowhere and discovering something beautiful—plus it helps me plan settings for my next book.

Socializing

I'm an introvert *and* an artist. "Socializing" is kind of a dirty word for me. But I've found that too much alone time gives me too much time to worry. Spending time with my loved ones and friends, regularly, helps me remember to live in the moment. Even if you don't have a lot of friends or a significant other, go to a bookstore or a coffee shop. Just get out and be around people once in a while—there *will* be someone, somewhere having a highly amusing conversation, at the very least.

Watching the Night Sky

Sometimes there's nothing better than lying on my back and watching the stars on a warm summer night. Need I say more? It's a cliché for a reason.

Accepting That Not Everyone Will Get It

Not everyone is going to understand. Some people will think I'm crazy, others will accuse me of being overly dramatic, and some just don't see it as a big deal. Plus, my anxiety can be a bitch to be around—I get it. But I'm done trying to hide it or saying I'm okay when I'm not. That only makes it harder to manage.

Knowing There's No Magic Cure— and Being Okay with It

I will always have anxiety—there are no magic medications or remedies. No special strawberries—although the Shuksans I picked in Washington came close. Just saying. My goal is to *keep living my life*. Focus on what I can do in this moment. How can I get through today? If anxiety gets the better of me again, that's okay. I give myself permission to fall down and get back up. But, for now, I'm going to try to follow the advice my very nonanxious husband always gives me.

"Worry about it when it happens."

Numb

by Kimberly McCreight

My first memory of feeling anxious is from around the time my parents divorced. I was eight years old, and suddenly I was terrified of dying. But—with Shakespearean flair—I wasn't just afraid of dying in general. I was specifically terrified that I would somehow accidentally poison myself with some otherwise innocuous household item.

Turns out most things we use every day could theoretically be fatal if you either a) eat them when you are not supposed to (e.g., cleaning products) or b) eat way more than you are supposed to (e.g., toothpaste). Trust the eight-year-old me. I had read all the labels.

If you are anxious yourself, the specificity of this may seem hilariously absurd and painfully familiar. For me, that is anxiety in a nutshell: as excruciating as it is ridiculous.

Almost funny. But only on a good day.

At the same time I also developed weird food aversions—I

can remember eating only lettuce for several months—and intense social phobia. These things were never addressed or treated or really even acknowledged. In my parents' defense, I did keep most of it a secret. Partly this was because I was confused and embarrassed and scared. I mean, I knew eating only lettuce—iceberg exclusively—wasn't what all the other kids were doing. I knew the other girls at my friend Caroline's birthday party didn't think that laundry detergent posed an imminent threat.

On the other hand, maybe someone should have inquired. I *was* eating only lettuce. But there was too much else going on. My family was falling apart, siblings being scattered to the four winds. Furniture was being divided. And there was all that rage to contend with, all those court dates to attend.

And so I did my best to hold it together on my own. Learn to live with a permanent knot in my stomach, to keep my lid screwed down tight. I was only eight years old, but I was already aware that there were many more pressing things than my worries. There were grown-ups who needed tending to.

Turns out all that practice swallowing down my undiagnosed feelings of unease made me pretty good at it. It even sort of worked for a pretty long time. I mean, I kept on keeping on. I survived. Happiness was a far spot on the horizon. But I was aces in the survival department.

In search of calmer waters, I eventually found my way to a boarding school. The stability there buoyed me somewhat. I got good grades and made a few friends. I was *always* still

168

anxious; I recognize that now. But at the time it didn't register as a problem, so much as simply the way I was. My social anxiety was probably the thing I noticed most because it kept me on the fringes of my high school social scene. If only I had known how lucky I was to be delaying my introduction to alcohol.

I didn't have my first drink until I was a junior in high school—a single wine cooler. A friend and I snuck them into my boarding school room on a rare weekend we stayed on campus. We drank them cross-legged on my dorm room floor. The whole thing was pretty uneventful except for the part where I walked into the bent front license plate of a parked car afterward and sliced open my bare calf. Not bad enough that I needed stitches—or not bad enough that I was forced to investigate whether I should get stitches—but all these years later I still have a hefty scar.

Perhaps I should have seen it as a bad omen. But how could I worry about signs when I had just learned how to fly?

I only really drank one other time in high school, though. The second time I was so eager for that sweet taste of freedom—freedom from me, from my worries—that I threw myself in with both feet.

It went less well. This time it was whiskey and Diet Coke, and I drank so much, so fast that I threw up and passed out on the bathroom floor of the house of someone I barely knew.

I was lucky, though. For starters, I didn't die. I bruised my chin where my face cracked down against the tile. But that was the worst of it. Or at least I think it was. I can't really be sure what happened that night. I blacked out for the first time.

The whole incident was enough to scare me straight for the rest of high school. It was clear: Alcohol and I weren't good together. We shouldn't be going steady. Shouldn't be friends with benefits. Actually, we should probably ignore the hell out of each other. So I retreated to the familiar—holding myself together, containing my panic through sheer force of will. And again it worked. Right up through graduation.

But once I got to college, all the carefully laid out methods I had of controlling my worry (which I still did not consider "anxiety," because no one had told me to) dissolved underfoot. Suddenly I was immersed in a world of no structure. Life was all about letting go and being free. Let me be clear: This did not feel like a bad thing. It was miraculous, thrilling. And all I wanted was to be able to keep up.

Luckily, I made incredible friends who were willing to serve as my guides in this exciting world of parties and boys and drama. There was just one stupid thing standing in the way: me.

But I already knew one surefire way to be free of me: alcohol. And lots and lots of it.

Drinking became my go-to solution, a quick-and-easy bridge between the anxious, socially phobic person I was and who I wanted to be: someone who didn't worry about everything all the time. Drinking got me so much closer to the happy, well-adjusted me of my imagination. And it gave me a much-needed break from myself.

Which, by the way, only seemed fair. If I was going to be plagued by so much worry, wasn't I entitled to an escape hatch? As a bonus, it was so much easier to talk to people when I was drunk. Three beers on any given Tuesday and off went the switch, down went the lights, and away went that weight that was always pressing on my chest. Not only didn't I feel worried anymore, I became the life of every party. I did things like tackle my freshman year roommate at a keg party and make up exotic, hilarious stories about a scar at my jaw-line. Or so I was told. I didn't actually remember any of it.

It's a common misperception that blacking out from drinking is the same thing as passing out. It is not. I have done both, and they are different, though both terrifying and dangerous and a clear sign that something in your relationship with alcohol is not right.

Passing out is when you drink so much you slip into a state of unconsciousness. Drinking enough so that you pass out can lead to various awful things, including death. When you black out, however, you can appear to be wide awake and functioning normally—talking to people, tackling them, making up lies about your scar—but not remember any of it.

By the second week of my freshman year, things were really going great. Or at least my social life was. I was fitting in, making more friends, having fun at parties six or seven nights a week.

True, I didn't remember most of it because I was blacking out so regularly, three or four (okay, maybe six) times a week.

Depending on how much and how quickly I drank, sometimes the blackouts took the form of loose ends. I wouldn't remember going to bed or there would be gaps in the chronology. But other times I drank enough that the entire night would be a terrifying, shameful black hole. Then I would have to rely on my friends to fill in what details they could.

This was all especially complicated where boys were concerned. I was also a bit of a late bloomer in the romance department (another consequence of all that anxiety). Sometimes it wasn't until someone approached me that I would even know that something had gone on between us. On one particular morning, I had a leftover flash of me and a boy I barely knew debating whether or not to steal a car. I believe this was my idea. (Luckily, we didn't do it).

Still, I thought I might be sick remembering it—this stranger who was me planning grand theft auto, willing to throw away everything she has worked for. This was the steep cost of many nights of freedom. Once the sun rose, my anxiety began demanding a full accounting.

Pretty soon much of each day was spent viciously hungover and—increasingly—unable to sit still. I couldn't take a deep breath for hours on end, heart racing as my thoughts spiraled away from me. Trying to remember what I had done. Trying to forget. This rebound effect was much worse than anything I had ever felt. I couldn't eat, couldn't focus. Couldn't think.

Drinking might be buying me nightly freedom, but it built a much more terrifying cage around my days.

Eventually, I did find my way into a counselor's office. In less than thirty seconds she told me that I was suffering from anxiety and was having panic attacks. And just having those words, that something to point to—I was elated. I felt almost like I was cured.

But there was no extended plan for therapy put in place. No medication prescribed. Not that I can necessarily blame my college counseling office. For all I know, these things were offered and I declined. I do not recall. The awful and sad truth is that I do not recall much of college now. Much less, it seems, than my friends, as though those years of blackouts have bled out and gobbled up the true memories that remained.

Nonetheless, the worst of my panic attacks did abate at the time, and I was left with the more ordinary dread I'd been living with for most of my life. It was then—for the first time—that I started to wonder whether constantly feeling like a concrete block was pressing down on my chest wasn't so normal after all. Because I had never really lived a "normal" life with "normal" people, what did I know about the way anyone was supposed to feel?

Meanwhile, I did keep on drinking. I mean, I figured if it wasn't totally broken, why fix it? True, bad things did keep happening, like losing my virginity and not being able to remember it.

But whatever. The first time you had sex was supposed to be awful for everyone anyway. Who wanted to remember? Right?

Yeah, not so much.

Not even I could convince myself of that. And so I decided to sober up. I figured if I stopped drinking for a while that maybe I could press the reset button. That I could start drinking again with more moderation. That the real problem wasn't why I was drinking—to escape my undiagnosed anxiety disorder—it was my lack of experience. My late start in life. I hadn't partied enough in high school, hadn't learned—like my more savvy friends—*how* to drink responsibly.

I forced myself to go out sober for at least a whole week. Or maybe it was more like five days. Five days that felt like five excruciating years. But I did it (okay, maybe it was only four days, but still). I had proved my point: I didn't *need* to drink. I could go out and socialize, could survive without it. And anyway, everyone else in college was drinking. Why should I, alone, have to suffer?

The answer? Because everyone else wasn't drinking like their life depended on it. They weren't drinking to survive.

I'd like to say that by my sophomore year in college I had found a terrific therapist and sobered up and begun to tackle the real problem of my underlying anxiety. God, how much I wish I could say that.

It would make me seem so much smarter and well adjusted.

But here's the thing: I was tragically good at being a drunk—things always got bad in a way that kept me from ever being happy, but not bad enough that I couldn't try to ignore it. Also I was really invested in there not being anything "wrong" with me (I guess having a drinking problem didn't count). I had held myself together for so long. I was afraid admitting there was a real problem would be like pulling a thread out of an old sweater. It would risk unraveling me down to my empty core.

Instead, I kept on using alcohol as an anxiety crutch in much the same way, for *years*. I would stop drinking whenever I hit a new, increasingly embarrassing rock bottom. Only to start up again. I did this through the rest of college. I did this through law school. I did this while I worked as a lawyer. I did this while I fell in love with my husband. And while I was off in London writing my first book.

And the whole time I was miserable and terrified and so completely and totally anxious. I was so much less free than I ever would have been sober. Than I could have been if I had poured even a tiny bit of the energy I put into yet another "get sober" plan into figuring out why I needed to drink in the first place.

For me, there was an answer. I was drinking because I was anxious. Because being drunk gave me the relief that I needed. Of course, the real tragedy is that without the alcohol I might have been forced to look my anxiety directly in the eye. To get the help I needed. To get to happy so much sooner.

I have been sober now for twelve years—the age of my older daughter. In the end, it took becoming a mother for me to get sober once and for all and to start facing the real things that I needed to work on. It is not easy not to drink. I accept that it may never be.

All these years later, I have used talk therapy and CBT (cognitive behavioral therapy) to help manage my anxiety. I have taken medication, and I meditate and exercise. And I accept that, for me, there may always be good days and bad days with my anxiety.

But today was a good day. Tomorrow? Who knows? I am still taking it one step at a time.

My Depression—
A Rock and a Hard Place

by Megan
Kelley Hall

It still visits me at times. I welcome it tentatively, like an old familiar friend. One that I feel comfortable around, whom I know inside and out. But one that has betrayed me again and again. One that I can never fully trust, because I've been burned before while being lulled into a false sense of security.

I've never viewed depression as an emotion. And not as something that has an end or a beginning. It just is. It has a shape and a weight. Not jagged or smooth. Not always big and not always small. Somewhere in between. Something hard and solid, like a rock. Sometimes it is as light as a pebble, able to be flicked off at the slightest notice. Sometimes it's ground into flecks of sand, barely noticeable and brushed away as quickly as it settles in. Other times it's a boulder with a crushing weight. One that feels immovable. Something you cannot get your arms around to move out of the way. And, at times, it is a mountain. An impossible obstacle in your path that you lack the energy to trek around, to climb over, or to tunnel beneath. And at the worst times, it may even beckon you to jump from its summit.

Though depression seemed to be passed down to me like a well-worn family heirloom, I wasn't destined for the darkness. Many are predisposed to the illness, and some depressions are brought on by circumstance. I got a healthy dose of both.

Following a lifetime of hospital visits—childhood cancer, back surgeries and a back brace in high school, premature birth in my twenties, heart surgeries in my thirties—depression easily forged a pathway into my life. Along with the health issues, there were the typical things that life throws at you: rejection in relationships, struggles in careers, death of family members and friends, betrayals, failed friendships, loss. Everyone experiences these things at varying levels of severity. The difference is that those with depression often find the simplest setbacks insurmountable.

And in my case, I had stress, anxiety, and panic attacks to put the cherry on top of my depression sundae. I struggled with all of those things on a daily basis growing up. In the eighties and nineties, Prozac was only a name on a book. Where the only people who talked about medication and depression were the characters in movies like *Girl, Interrupted* and *Reality Bites*. All of life's problems could be cleared up in a half-hour sitcom with a recycled laugh track or on the beaches of 90210. Back then people just didn't talk about depression for fear of being called "crazy."

During my sophomore year of college, my father had a heart attack, my first real boyfriend broke up with me, and my best friend betrayed me and turned all my friends against me. It was a horrible winter in upstate New York with multiple feet of snow, and I was totally isolated from friends and family. I expressed feelings of despair to a friend who was also an RA, and due to my flair for the dramatic, I was suddenly forced into therapy with the school psychologist. They feared I'd do something drastic. Something that would be a splotch of darkness on their colorful college catalog. Depression was something that needed to be attacked head-on and eradicated.

My one and only counseling session ended in a threat to call my parents if I didn't notify them on my own. I was told that a student could get kicked out if he or she had thoughts of suicide. (I didn't.) And that as a member of student government, I would be a bad example. (I wasn't.) My dad had just survived death and I had overcome cancer as a child. The last thing on my mind was ending my own life. Sure, I didn't mind hurting myself by smoking too many cigarettes and staying up all night and notching up the angst level to the highest decibels, but I was grateful to be alive, despite the fact that it felt like life sucked in every conceivable way. So I told the therapist that I would come clean to my parents. (I wouldn't.)

Depression in the nineties was something alien to administrators, to those who came of age in the free-loving, tie-dyed seventies or the preppy, Reaganomic eighties. We were the Nirvana grunge era. The whiskey-soaked cries from Pearl Jam and Soundgarden that funneled through my Sony Discman were the perfect embodiment of the ennui and malaise I felt. Why wasn't I out there sunning myself on the quad with my peers? Didn't I know that these were the best days of my life? What was wrong with me? Why couldn't I just cheer up?

So I struggled with all of it on my own, hid it like a dirty little secret, and everything suffered: my grades, my health, my social life, my self-esteem. I kept it from my family because after my dad's heart attack I didn't want to be any more of a burden than I already was. My college education cost nearly one hundred grand, and I (wrongly) believed that this financial burden contributed to my dad's poor health.

As far as I was concerned, I wasn't allowed to be depressed. Not only was I alienated at school for suffering from it, but I had no good reason for it. (At least that's what I kept telling myself.) I was lucky! I was getting a good education at a great school. I had my whole life ahead of me! I had kicked cancer's butt as a kid. I was a warrior! But I was going through a series of life-altering situations, and I was still in my teens. I was unmedicated, isolated, and my emotions were raw, exposed, and dragged around for everyone to see.

Almost two decades later it's evident that things have changed. Not only has the Internet connected the world and reality TV brought every dark little secret we all felt as exclusively ours to light, but a mental disorder like depression isn't something to be ashamed of or to keep hidden from the world—it never was. These days you'd be hard-pressed to find someone who doesn't live with some form of mental illness, whether it be anxiety attacks, PTSD, OCD, bipolar disorder, or simply mild depression. Yet when the depression rolled into my life like a massive boulder, I wasn't prepared for it. I hid it. I ignored it. I rolled it into the corner and threw my clothes on top of it. I pretended it didn't exist. I tried chipping away at it with the only useless tools at my disposal—as ineffective as a nail file, when what I needed was a jackhammer.

But since then I've realized that depression can strike at any time. It can come on like a hailstorm in the middle of a beautiful sunny day. I've learned to control it through medication, yoga and meditation, exercise, and really good talks with people who care about me. Yet, even with all of those things in reserve, nothing completely keeps my depression from rearing its ugly head. It pops up at times when I should be at my happiest—on vacation in Hawaii, signing a contract for a book deal, a fun night out with family and friends. There is no warning for when that familiar bag of rocks lands at my door, unannounced and unwelcome.

But these days I have enough tools in my arsenal as well as instructions for how to deal with those setbacks. You never really rid yourself of depression, in the same way that those old friends you wish would be out of your life forever keep popping in to say hello. To remind you of times when you weren't in total control. To remind you of the pressure you endured. But you learn to manage, to work around them, to accept them for what they are and not let them weigh you down. To show them that they have no power over you.

Not anymore.

There will always be sunny, carefree days when everything is right with the world, and there will also inevitably be the dark ones. The difference is how you choose to view them. Living with depression can feel like carrying a big, immovable rock. But without great pressure and a handful of volatile eruptions, life can never reach its full potential of becoming a strong and beautiful diamond.

Everything and Anything

by Hannah Moskowitz

I like to read about plane crashes while I'm waiting at the airport. I sit in the food court and read about black-box recorders and engine failures and mountains appearing out of nowhere. For some reason it calms me down. I want to know what the worst thing is that can happen. When I get on board and they ask if anyone's uncomfortable sitting in the emergency exit row, I think about how freaking fantastic I would be sitting next to that door, if it came to it. I might suck at everyday existence—I cry over the dishes, I stall scooping the litter box, and I never, ever leave the house on time—but I would be amazing in a plane crash. It's the bonus of having anxiety and paranoia amped up to eleven at all times. I'm used to feeling like I'm crashing.

I've read every Wikipedia entry on serial killers and every Snopes article on freak accidents. I know all the amusement park deaths. I know who the first person was to be killed by an escalator. I know the symptoms of diseases you've never heard of. I go on kitten-rearing forums and only read the topic where it warns you that the cat dies at the end.

I like my fanfic bloody and sad. I'll read just about anything with self-injury or eating disorders, both issues I've dealt with in my past, and in fact I've written a book about each. Give me your horrifying, your tragic, your irredeemably bleak; I'm not afraid. It's not that I want these things to happen, it's just that whether or not I read about them, they're still there. It's the same reason I don't understand writers who don't look at their royalty statements or people who dread getting report cards. Whether or not you know the information doesn't mean it isn't there. Wouldn't you feel better if you just knew?

So I read about everything, and I'll write about anything.

Except for one thing. I don't read about bipolar disorder, and this is my first time writing about it.

I actively avoid it. It doesn't matter who's writing it. My lord and savior E. Lockhart could write a bipolar main character and I wouldn't read it. I don't care whether or not the writer has bipolar disorder, or has a family member with it. My issue isn't that it won't feel realistic, because the truth is, with mental illness, there is no true realistic and unrealistic. Every symptom you haven't had, someone else with your same diagnosis has. And no edition of the *Diagnostic and Statistical Manual* is ever going to have a good description of what the particular bug in your particular brain feels like, how the scratch scratch scratching sounds, how the little claw kneads in and out and in and out while you're trying to sleep.

I don't want to read anyone else describing that.

The fact that it's hard and probably impossible for a mental illness depiction to actually *be* inauthentic doesn't keep it from feeling inauthentic—kind of the opposite, really. Because nobody's mental illness is the same, no representation is ever going to ring 100 percent true to you. To me. And because fiction has to have conflict, drama, and interest, mental illness is often portrayed in the most dynamic, explosive way possible.

When I'm talking about—when I'm *forced* to talk about— bipolar disorder to someone, I usually tell them that it's boring. And it's true. The vast majority of days, my bipolar disorder, thankfully, doesn't determine much about my life. I have to worry about health insurance all the time, and I'm always, always checking in with myself (I don't have bad moods—I have bad moods with a side of *but are you sure you're not getting depressed?*), but for the most part my bipolar disorder draws attention to itself for ten seconds once a day when I take my meds. It wasn't always like that, but now, with six years of treatment under my belt, things are pretty stable. What's bipolar disorder like? It's boring.

Except, you know, when it's not. But that's not part of my sound bite.

The bipolar characters that I have seen, that I guilt myself into reading or that surprise me on my TV screen, tend to have a backstory that's very different from mine. This is something

I see time and time again in depictions of any mental illness: The character always says *there's nothing wrong with me.* It's always everyone else who has the problem. They're fine. They're *normal.*

So . . . am I the only person on earth who's known for as long as she can remember that something was not right? That it should not have been this hard? I couldn't have been less surprised by my bipolar diagnosis. I'd just been waiting until I had the courage to go to a psychiatrist. I was putting it off because I was scared—remember how I postpone things that scare the shit out of me, like doing the dishes or leaving my apartment?—not because I was in denial that I had a problem.

But these characters: they're fine, they're normal, everyone's making a big deal out of nothing, and then there's a breaking point and they end up in the psych ward. And that's where they get diagnosed, not in some psychiatrist's office on the fourth floor of an office building in suburban Maryland.

Let's go back to the plane-crash stories.

It's about feeling prepared, sure, but it's also kind of a rush, because these people were *just like me.* They were hanging out at the airport, eating Sbarro, their three-ounce liquids in ziplocks, their boarding passes tucked away. But they had no idea what was going to happen, and I did. I know everything that can happen to people like us.

And then enter bipolar disorder, and these characters who aren't just like me, who don't have my backstory. They're not hanging out at the airport with me. They're jumping out of planes.

186

The truth is, sometimes it gets really bad.

Sometimes I just really want to know how it's going to turn out. And sometimes I really, really don't. But either way, the stories aren't going to help me. Those characters aren't like me. They're *totally normal*. They're *totally fine*.

I am totally not.

All plane crashes are pretty much the same. And all mentally ill people could not be more different. If I read stories and see what happens to them, it reminds me that I have no idea what's going to happen to me. I can't prepare for this. I don't know everything that can happen to people like me.

So I take my meds and get ready to be struck by lightning, or to get stuck in a car underwater, or to be swallowed up by a tornado (I know what to do with all of these).

I know what to do.

I know what to do.

Better Than Normal

by Karen Mahoney

Here is what I want to tell you: I have suffered with severe anxiety for pretty much my entire life. I have good days and bad days. I've had terrible days and weeks and months at a time when I am seriously ill. I've also had days and weeks and months at a time when I am mostly okay (often—though not always—thanks to medication).

But here is what I *need* to tell you: I've survived. I survive every single day. I will never give up. And if you are suffering, whether with some form of anxiety disorder or any number of other mental health problems, you can survive too. I know it because I have lived it, and I'm still here. We can do this together.

I am not a mental health professional, and if you are suffering in silence with any of these things, I strongly urge you to seek help and advice because that help and advice is available. I know it's hard. I really, really do know that. It took me a long time to reach out beyond the circle of my immediate family. But, trust me, things are getting better as far as treating mental health is concerned—and you can get better too. Maybe not exactly "cured," but you can live a good life. You can learn coping mechanisms. You can take the right meds (if you even need them, because not everybody does) and try different therapies and learn self-care that takes into account your own, unique form of mental illness—because we are all different, and we all suffer in weird and wonderful and different ways.

So no, I am not an expert on these matters. But I am an expert on my *own* life and experiences. And that is what I want to share with you here. Maybe it will help. Maybe not, but at least it might entertain you? Because I tend to use humor to distract from my pain, and if nothing else, that can be entertaining in a reality-TV kind of way.

I hardly ever talk about this stuff. In fact, I seem to have made it my life's mission to hide the truth of my condition from a great many people. That stops today because I have nothing to be ashamed of. None of us do. This is a much-needed conversation in our society, and I am so glad that we are having it.

Only recently, Kristen Bell talked openly about her experiences with mental illness and medication. Zayn Malik pulled out of a major gig because of his ongoing struggle with anxiety. I find this willingness to be vulnerable so inspiring. I admire those people in the public eye who step forward and speak up on these issues, because it helps others (the not-famous people) to say "Me too" without shame. Like I'm doing now.

Honestly, I am more relieved than anything else, because it's bloody exhausting pretending to be normal all the time.

I was twenty-seven when I had my first nervous breakdown.

I say "nervous breakdown" because, dramatic as it sounds, that's what it was called at the time by the emergency psychiatrist I saw. The term "nervous breakdown" is somewhat outdated now, but the meaning remains the same: My nerves just . . . broke down. Completely and utterly. I was almost hospitalized, and the only reason I was allowed to go home that day was because I had family who could vouch for my safety.

I left the hospital with a prescription for three separate medications:

- A tranquilizer—for immediate relief.
- A beta blocker—for midterm management.
- An antidepressant—for long-term treatment.

I was a mess. I was confused. I was terrified. But hey, look on the bright side: At least I wasn't prescribed antipsychotic medication, right? Oh, except I *was* prescribed those very things several years later. Apparently antipsychotics can be used short term to treat severe anxiety. Who knew? Not me—although I certainly do now! (Actually, I originally had a whole amusing anecdote about the first time I was given antipsych meds by my doctor but decided to cut it for space. If this were a DVD rather than an essay, I could include it in the deleted scenes section, along with the story of how I got bitten by a squirrel and thought I might turn into Squirrel Girl. Ah well. Maybe next time . . .)

Over the years the closest diagnosis we've reached—because diagnosing mental health issues is not always an exact science—is that I have chronic anxiety (including both social anxiety and generalized anxiety disorders) and panic disorder. Oh, and a side helping of trichotillomania. Don't worry, we'll be getting to that.

Back then, however, it was early days with all this—at least as far as an actual diagnosis was concerned. Sure, I knew there was anxiety involved, because I'd been "sensitive" and anxious for what seemed like forever, but this was capital-A anxiety. The kind of anxiety that can ruin both your relationships and the ability to hold down a job. The kind that makes you genuinely question your sanity and believe that maybe you are irreparably broken. Now that I am better able to understand things like adrenaline overload and the fight-or-flight response, it seems less scary. Well, theoretically. The reality of each relapse is still scary as shit.

I had ongoing panic attacks that hit me first thing in the morning—very early, jolting me awake and leaving me pinned to the bed for hours, sweating and shaking with my heart pounding, all alone until the rest of the house was awake—a sense of very real terror, *physiological* terror, that kept going for most of the day, gradually winding down toward evening, so I got a small measure of relief before going to bed, trying and failing to sleep until the early hours, and then waking up to do it all over again.

The thing I hate the most when I am going through one of the more serious episodes is that I can't really *do* anything— it is very hard to take my mind off the constant activity in my nervous system that keeps me buzzing on high alert. I remember, in my twenties, when I realized that I couldn't even read—the thing I loved to do most in the world—and I found it devastating. The lines of text seemed to slide down the page, and I felt more and more anxious the longer I tried to capture the words, words that just kept running away. It was my mum who suggested I try doing jigsaw puzzles because they gave me something sort of mindless-but-ordered to focus on. I was exhausted after putting together one corner, but it worked. There I was, as a young adult, living with my parents and doing jigsaw puzzles in order to stay sane.

One day, while very early on in my recovery, I tried taking a bath by myself. This was a huge deal at the time. My mum kept calling up the stairs, periodically, to check I was okay. She wouldn't allow me to lock the door, which turned out to be a good thing, because, long after I had supposedly gotten out and dressed, she found me on the bathroom floor, curled up in a damp robe, just staring at the wall. I hardly remember it.

She got me into bed and sat with me, trying to get me to snap out of it—whatever "it" was. I was certain I was dying because of all the awful physical sensations running through my body.

My mum said, "You're not dying."

"Are you sure?" I kept asking her. "Are you sure?"

"I'm sure."

"But *how*? How can you be sure?"

"I just am. You're going to be fine. You are going to get better." Stroking my hair just like when I was sick as a child.

Even today I hate that I put my mum through that when I was supposed to be an adult making my way in the world. Of course I know much better now that I couldn't help it. It absolutely wasn't—and isn't—my fault. And yet the guilt still lingers. Why is it that mental illness leaves its sufferers feeling *guilty* for something that is genuinely beyond their control? I constantly felt like an invalid—only I was an "invalid" with no external signs of illness or injury to show for all the suffering and pain I was inflicting on myself and everyone else, sitting in a rocking chair, wrapped in a blanket despite the mild temperature, staring out the patio-door windows at the garden. Waiting for the sun to come out again.

Historically, I can trace my problems with anxiety all the way back to early childhood. I've often found myself looking for answers—trying to make meaning out of the illness I've experienced for so many years. Trying to get to the bottom of why I am like this. My investigation has unearthed *some* evidence that hints at the very early roots of the problem, but no real answers as to *why*.

Here, for example, is the very first paragraph of my very first school report when I was just seven years old:

Karen is a very competent girl. She is a pleasant member of the class. Karen is an anxious girl and often seeks reassurance. Karen worries about events before they happen.

Hmm . . . On the plus side (hey, look, budding writer!):

Her creative writing is promising. The content is interesting and her spelling is good.

Although,

Her presentation is variable; Karen must try to stabilise her style of handwriting.

(Sadly, my handwriting never did stabilize. You can ask my boyfriend about this for corroboration. I still write like a seven-year-old.)

The following year, now aged eight:

Karen has worked hard all year, but she needs to take a less anxious approach to school work.

Easier said than done, my friend. Easier said than done. But, as usual, there was always this silver lining:

Karen enjoys writing in particular and her stories are a pleasure to read.

Yay?

It goes on. By the start of what we in the UK call secondary school (now aged eleven), my tutor ended her glowing report with:

Although I feel she is occasionally overanxious, on the whole Karen seems happy and well-settled.

"Occasionally overanxious" could be something of an understatement, considering that on my very first day of my new, grown-up school, wearing my new grown-up-school uniform, after my mum had dropped me off right at the gates and given me an awesome pep talk because she knew how nervous I was feeling . . . I promptly threw up all over my brand-new shoes. In the street. Right there, in front of everyone. It was not my finest moment. My poor mum had to take me into the school bathroom and clean me up as best she could.

As usual, once I'd been *physically* sick, I actually felt much better, though I was horribly aware of the faint smell of vomit lingering around me for the rest of the day, making it hard for me to feel good about trying to make friends. I kept worrying about who had seen me throw up. Would I be known as Puke Girl for my entire secondary-school career? (Luckily, that didn't happen.)

The thing is, the combination of school and throwing up was already a familiar scenario for me. Remember those report comments about my anxiety when I was just seven? The previous year I had been so scared of my teacher that I was physically sick every single morning before leaving for school. To begin with, my mum was of course concerned and took me to the doctor. Eventually, however, it just became routine: force down some cereal, despite feeling nauseous, throw up in the kitchen sink (already cleared of dishes by my super-prepared mum), then go to school as though nothing had happened. It was bizarrely normal for us. The doctor said

I was suffering "nerves" and that I had a "nervous tummy." I don't think we really had the language to talk about serious anxiety disorders back then, and certainly not in such a young child.

Mental illnesses tend to hunt in packs. Especially, in my experience, when it comes to anxiety disorders. If you have one, you will invariably have at least another in a kind of twisted buy-one-get-one-for-free deal. (BOGOFF is exactly what I want to tell all *my* various disorders, but even when I do, they rarely listen.)

So, yes. A delightful consequence (side effect?) of my condition has been developing *other* conditions. My particular specialty is trichotillomania. Or trich, as sufferers call it. Also referred to as TTM in the DSM-V, the cheery medical handbook for all mental illness sufferers. See? I told you we'd get to the juicy stuff.

Trichotillo-WHAT? I hear some of you ask. I don't blame you, because that was me at one time. Although I feel pretty sure there will be some fellow sufferers out there reading this (waves to fellow trichsters), it took me a long time to even realize this is an actual condition. Trichotillomania is a body-focused repetitive behavior. An impulse-control disorder that involves pulling out your own hair. Some studies link it directly to OCD, and it definitely appears to be anxiety- and stress-related. My thing? Eyelashes. It is surprisingly common, especially among teens. I hid it well to begin with, exercising willpower so that I would only pull out a small amount and leave just enough that I could do a decent cover-up job with mascara and eyeliner. But as I have gotten older, things have escalated. Sometimes I can go long periods of time without pulling at all. But there are other times when I can't seem to stop. Times when my loving-but-long-suffering boyfriend seems to be constantly grabbing my hand away from my face while we're watching something on TV:

"Can you not do that during *Game of Thrones?* The movement keeps catching my eye. It's really distracting!"

"I can't help it!"

"I know, but maybe you could try to hold off until we're watching something less intense."

"It's called an *impulse-control* disorder for a reason, thank you very much. My disorder doesn't discriminate between TV shows."

Dermatillomania, or skin-picking disorder, is a related condition. I've gone through phases of that, too. At the risk of going all TMI and grossing you out (sorry!), I once picked the heel of my left foot so badly that I left bloody footprints on the kitchen floor. I couldn't walk properly for several days and had to tell people I had "really bad blisters." There are some studies that draw comparisons between these body-focused compulsions and self-harm, and, sadly, that makes a lot of sense.

My tendency to relapse into trich and trich-related behaviors is definitely linked to my anxiety levels. Half the time I am not even aware that I'm doing it, so that isn't awesome.

There is no cure, although sometimes medication and cognitive therapy can help. The only way I've personally found to deal with it is to simply try hard to be conscious of where my hands are at all times. Given the whole lack-of-awareness thing I just mentioned, this is easier said than done. There are a lot of *trichs* (ha! See what I did there?) that sufferers can try, and you can find all kinds of great information, forums, and communities online these days. You are not alone. I actually get bizarrely excited when I hear about someone famous who has suffered from trichotillomania. And the first time I saw Diablo Cody's film *Young Adult* (starring Charlize Theron), I was shocked—in a good way—to see the main character pulling at her hair so much that she has to cover up bald spots with a blond hairpiece. I've never pulled the hair on my head, but it's all part of the same condition. The more we see that we're maybe not quite as weird as we thought, the more validated and empowered we will be.

Okay, it's probably still pretty weird, but at least we're not alone.

Over the years I've learned that anxiety disorders are quite hard for "normal" people to understand. I have to point out here that I don't blame those people. At all. If I blame anything, I suppose I'd focus more on the stigma in general that surrounds mental health problems in our society. Thankfully, things are improving, although there is still work to be done. In the earlier days of my illness, when people first discovered what was going on with me—often because I had no choice but to reveal it as I was, once again, off sick from one of my many jobs and the Awful Truth had come out—they were confused. Sometimes the best reaction I can still hope for is a sort of bemused kindness.

People say things like, "So . . . you worry about stuff?"

And I am like, "It's more than that. I actually can't function when I get really bad."

"Because . . . you get *anxious*? How does that stop you functioning? I mean, everyone worries, don't they?"

Yes, I want to say. Of course a certain level of anxiety is normal, and even desirable in terms of keeping us safe from genuine danger. But not everyone has to crawl from the bedroom to the bathroom because standing is too difficult. Not everyone wakes up *every . . . single . . . morning*, usually around five a.m., with adrenaline coursing through their body. Not everyone sleeps only two or three hours a night, can hardly eat without puking, and has to turn off the TV because the colors are too bright.

Anxiety disorders can be punishing, man.

And I find it exhausting to try explaining that to the people who aren't listening anyway. They don't *really* care. They just want to know when you're coming back to work and whether you're crazy or not. They're wondering whether they can get rid of you somehow without getting sued for constructive dismissal.

On the other hand there are people who at least *try* to get it and who absolutely do care. People who say things like, "I may not really understand what you're going through, but I can see how very ill you get, and I want you to get better."

That genuinely helps, and I am so thankful for those kinds of responses.

If you are having trouble finding helpful voices in your life (and I'm not talking about the ones in your head), listen, instead, to your fellow sufferers. Listen to the people who love you: your family and true friends. Listen to your doctor or therapist. Hell, listen to me! Or to any of the authors of the essays in this book. Listen when I tell you that you are a worthwhile human being and it's so important that you are in this world. I have honestly come to believe that the most interesting of us have been broken and patched up, time and time again. You are needed. And loved. Your existence matters. Your illness does not define you, and things *will* get better.

Having a chronic anxiety disorder has messed with my life for sure. It sucks. I'm not going to say that it doesn't. But I wouldn't change it, not now. Too many years have passed, and I have learned so much—about myself, about other people and their attitudes to mental illness, and also about how there are some wonderful people who are always willing to help. I am so lucky to have a partner who accepts me with all of my neuroses and (*ahem*) character quirks and odd phobias . . . who values me and the person I truly am, not just despite those quirks but *because* of them. (Okay, he just read this and said maybe that last part is going too far. But whatever. He's stuck with me now!)

It's not easy living with any kind of chronic illness. At times I still struggle with feelings of shame and failure. Sometimes I feel like a fraud because I know people with what I *still* can't help describing as "real" chronic illnesses—physical illnesses that have actually visible signs. And then I remind myself that it is not a competition and that I am allowed to be sick. That I can't help it, although I can help myself by seeking out medical care and support. I can try to live a healthier life. This last one, I have to admit, I am not very good at. I drink too much caffeine and eat too much sugar. I could do with exercising more, because that is something that definitely helps. I do find that simply walking with the sun on my face can lift my mood so much that it is almost a bloody miracle. (Of course, that is assuming I feel psychologically up to leaving the house at all that day.) I hide away far too much, and that is something I need to work on—although it is also important that we are not so hard on ourselves. We are not living in a video game, no matter how much we might like playing them. Our mental health is not a brightly colored life bar on a screen that we are irreversibly consuming. Self-care is important.

These days I try to practice a form of radical self-acceptance which comes down to this: I may not ever "get over" my various disorders, but I can learn to live with them.

My mother and my partner do not suffer from mental health problems themselves, but they have contributed to saving my life. I believe that with all my heart. The other thing that has saved me is writing. I don't think I would be a writer without my anxiety, which might sound strange but is no less true for all that. So thanks for listening to my rambling here. If you take nothing else from this essay, I'd like you to remember these words—my mum's words to me one time when I was crying and in total despair about ever getting better, and I told her that I was afraid I would never be normal.

"Normal? Well . . ." My mum shook her head, smiling fondly. (Or possibly she was grimacing. I don't fully recall.) "You've never really been normal. Why start now?"

"Oh, thanks a *lot*."

"Seriously, though," Mum continued. "What *is* normal? What does that even mean?"

I sniffled and looked at her, wondering what she was talking about. "But I want to be normal!"

"Why on *earth* would you want to be something as boring as *normal*?" she replied. "You're better than normal."

So rock your weirdness. Fly your freak flag. Be yourself, no matter what your flavor of mental illness. Who cares about normal?

We're *better* than normal.

What If?

by Tom Pollock

Alarm goes. Wake up. Clock radio burbles.

Get up.

Get *up.*

Why haven't you gotten up yet?

What if you can't? What if it's finally come—the day you can't manage it, and that paves the way for tomorrow, and that paves the way for the day after that, and getting up becomes a kind of distant, golden memory that you suspect might have always been a myth, and you never get out of bed again, and your body slowly liquefies into the mattress like a cucumber that's been left in the fridge for six months?

Okay, you're up.

Check Twitter. Aw, cute kitty! Shower. Brush teeth. Get dressed. Accidentally almost step on cat. Cat explodes out from under foot like yowling black land mine. Perform awkward hopping with one leg in trouser in attempt to regain balance. Fail. *Thunk*. Ow. Cat approaches cautiously, but then licks bruised head. Apparently you're forgiven. Sorry, cat.

Leave house. Board bus. Did you close the door behind you? Yes. Of course you did; you ALWAYS close the door behind you; why would today be any different?

. . . but what if you didn't?

Seriously, you want to go back? Okay, fine. But make it quick.

Get off bus. Run back down street to house. Door certainly *looks* shut. Open it and close it again to make sure. Definitely shut. Definitely. Turn to go. Argh, did you shut it? You have a *memory* of shutting it, but now you're not sure if that memory is from today or yesterday, or any of the other eleventy billion times you've shut this door. Physically turn around and around and around on yourself while deciding whether to go back and check again. Know you won't have any peace until you do. Go back. Open it, close it, go through that weird ritual of pushing on all four panels on it first clockwise, then counterclockwise— that seems to help. Exhale hard. It's closed. Remember it.

Board new bus. Dig out Kindle and start to read. Worry that you don't read enough, you're supposed to be a writer, after all, and you need to feed the synthesis machine. Get distracted, check Twitter. Aw, cute puppy! Berate self for getting distracted. This is why you don't read enough. Back to reading. It's a thriller, a good one. Bet the husband did it, though; that's in vogue right now. Besides he's a douchebag, and it's suspicious that no one suspects him.

Arrive at train station. You're so late now. Wait on platform. *Please stand clear of the platform edge; the next train is not scheduled to stop at this station.* The 7:58 express to Reading is charging up toward you, huge and fast and full of momentum. . . .

—just for a split second, think about jumping in front of it—

Nope, too late, it's past. You can feel the vacuum in its wake sucking at your clothes. Can other people on the platform tell you're shaking against the inside of your trouser legs? Probably not.

You're a big lad with a shaved head. Big lads with shaved heads do not think like this in the popular imagination, which is probably part of why you shave your head and spend two afternoons a week picking up heavy bits of metal and putting them down again. Dress for the job you want and all that. . . .

Your train comes. Board it. Check Twitter, aw SLOTH IN A CAPTAIN AMERICA OUTFIT!

Get to work. Do work. Smile and laugh and chat with colleagues at coffee machine. Wonder if any of them ever think about jumping in front of trains. Probably most people do at some point, don't they? In a tentative attempt to secure common ground, show them Captain America Sloth on your phone. Receive only odd looks. Contemplate the insularity of the geek bubble on the Internet that you call home.

Do more work. Try to work out what a nuclear meltdown, a financial crisis, and an oil platform blowing up have in common. Interesting—scary, though—people seem incapable of asking for help at the right time, even when they know they need it, too scared of people judging them, apparently. The moral-of-the-story Klaxon goes off in your head, but it's cut short by your boss, calling you into an office.

Uh-oh, he wants to give you feedback. This can't be good. Oh! It *is* good. It's good feedback. Feel good. Feel proud. Worry slightly that this pride will inevitably lead to a hideous death spiral of complacency, torpor, and failure, but that's for later. Now: *proud*.

Go back to desk. Reply to e-mail from friend. Friend replies to your reply. Friend is angry. Friend has misinterpreted your e-mail. Friend thinks you're a bad friend. You *are* a bad friend. You've let them down. Completely forget that this is all a misunderstanding based on ambiguous word choice in your first e-mail: You weren't considerate enough of their feelings. They probably hate you. You would, if you were them. Work pride has now dissolved like a sugar cube in a flushing toilet. You're a thoughtless, worthless, callous, stupid . . .

Oh great, *here* we go.

Off to the shop, then the cafeteria, then the vending machine. Kit Kat, chicken-and-bacon baguette, donut, three apples, Maltesers, tuna pasta salad; teeth working and tearing, chew, swallow, chew, swallow. *She cannae do it, Cap'n; she will nae take the strain!* No choice, Mr. Scott— eat eat *eat*.

Drenched in sweat now. Shop, caf, vending machine: a tight

little circuit that's just on the verge of breaking into a run. You rotate the places you buy the food so as not to attract attention, but at this rate it hardly matters; you'll be on your third trip round in no time.

Mars bar, chips—what flavor? Can't remember—supermarket sushi mashing together in your mouth with Skittles and handfuls of dry pasta from the office kitchen and Diet Coke bubbles bursting in your throat and eat eat EAT. It's not quite automatic, not quite without pause. Every now and then you hesitate, consider. You try to tell yourself:

Stop. What are you doing? This won't help anything. You can stop.

And you can. The problem is you know that the second after that you can start eating again. And if by some miracle of self-restraint you hold out, then the second after *that* you'll have another chance to eat again, and so on and so on: an endless parade of moments of decision, and having the strength to make the right choice in all of those moments seems impossible. That would require—mathematically—an infinite reserve of mental energy, and right now you barely have enough to form this thought.

So you eat, mostly to get it over with, because you know you can't bind the *you* who will exist two seconds from now, and you sure as hell don't trust that stranger.

Later—belly fully of sugar and shame—you'll run. Eight, ten, twelve miles, some push-ups, some burpees, not nearly enough to offset the ludicrous number of calories you consumed, but a kind of down payment, a nibble at the corner of the vast debt you've incurred on yourself.

At some point you find an empty meeting room and curl up on the floor counting your breaths.

At fifty, you tell yourself, you'll get up. *Forty-eight, forty-nine, fifty.* Hey! You did get up. Go, you! Okay, go back to your desk. Try to work. Nope, you can't concentrate. You wonder if your colleagues will notice how you're sweating, how you keep typing the same handful of words over and over and then deleting them.

At some point you go for a walk outside; you're still struggling to catch your breath. Without really thinking about why, you cross the parking lot to the new building. It's lovely and sunny. You smile at the receptionist at the desk and jog up the stairs. The new building is built around a big open atrium, glass roofed, light and airy. Five floors in total and every one of them has an internal balcony.

You stand at the top one, maybe eighty feet up? The railing's only two feet high; you brace your arms against it and look down. If anyone passes, it looks like you're just leaning on it enjoying the view, but you're acutely aware of how your weight's just a *little* far forward, that you're up on the balls of your feet, knees slightly bent, minimizing the effort that would be needed to flip your center of gravity up over your hands, swing your briefly weightless body out past the railing, and then drop like a stone.

It's definitely high enough, especially if you make sure you fall headfirst. You know; you looked it up.

The thing no one tells you about suicidal thoughts is that they're a habit, and like most bad habits they get harder and harder to break as you indulge them.

In a lot of ways, wanting to kill yourself feels like being on a diet and being surrounded by plump, delicious donuts glistening with sugar and bursting with jam. You know you shouldn't give in. You know eating the donut won't make you any happier in the long run. You know the satisfaction will be infinitesimally short and the regret will be instantaneous and lasting. But you also know that if you decide not to give in now, then you'll be able to change your mind the next instant, and the next after that. The temptation will just keep hanging over you until eventually you cave, just to relieve the pressure, and if, as you demonstrated an hour ago, in the face of that pressure, you can't stop yourself from indiscriminately shoving food in your face, where on earth are you going to get the self-control to keep yourself from jumping off the nearest precipice when the mood takes you?

Breathe out, slowly. Remind yourself that you love your wife, your sister, your family. Think about what this would do to them. That's always been your break-glass-in-case-of-emergency self-preservation technique, and here again, it works wonders.

Besides, you're still here. You've felt like this loads of times, and you haven't acted on it yet. It might not feel like it, but it *is* different from the binge eating. You're a diagnosed bulimic—lots of people are; doesn't mean they all go around offing themselves in random spasms of untameable impulse. Get a grip.

Still, to be safe, better get away from temptation. You jog back down the steps and smile at the receptionist again on the way out.

Go home early, telling your boss you have a headache, which, after all, is literally true, if not explanatory. Interestingly, you feel no urge at all to jump in front of the train as it arrives. Also like a lot of bad habits, indulging in a suicidal thought will tide you over, for a while.

You get home and order pizza, because the diet is fucked today anyway, and check Twitter. Hey, cute baby ostrich! Briefly wonder if you should follow something other than cute animal accounts on Twitter. Laugh. Follow six more cute animal accounts on Twitter.

Your wife gets home; you ask her how her day was. "Fine," she says. "You?"

"Same," you reply.

You spend the night together on the sofa watching *Brooklyn Nine-Nine*. She laughs, and that's it. You're happy. You want to spend eternity listening to her laugh, and you married her because you figured that the rest of your life was the next best thing. You are happy now. Deeply and deliriously content. Remember this moment. Enjoy it, sure, but also fix it in your memory, because this is what's going to make the difference the next time you encounter a high place or a sharp edge or a heavy, fast-moving object. It's a cliché, but it's true: When you're depressed, it feels like that's how you always feel, how you *will* always feel, but that's a lie; this moment is the proof of it. Seal it behind glass for the next time you need it.

And then worry, like you always do, that next time it might not be enough, that you might forget, or flail and panic and act before you can get your head in order. That future you, wild, unpredictable and utterly beyond your power, could get up in the night, go to the knife rack in the kitchen, betray this moment and her, and there will be nothing that present you can do about it.

But then, that's always been the danger, hasn't it? It's *always* been true that future-you was someone else. All our future selves are. We never know for sure what they're going to do. The only reason we have to trust in them is the same reason we have to trust in anyone, in any*thing*: that it's been there for us in the past.

To put it another way, if you believe the sun's coming up tomorrow, you have every reason to believe you'll be around to see it.

Speaking of which, it's bedtime. It's been a tiring day. Get undressed. Brush your teeth. Check Twitter. Hey, cute panda!

Try to sleep.

Objects in the Mirror . . .

by Cyn Balog

If you're like me, you know the drill.

You wake up at four in the morning because it takes just that long to get ready, to make yourself halfway presentable. You can't skip a step in your morning routine, or else everyone will notice. You stare at your reflection in mirrors, the backs of spoons, windows, soap bubbles, car fenders, whatever. Whenever you do, you always cringe. Not good enough. Even your best is not good enough. People must see those flaws, and that's why they hate you. They don't say that, but maybe they looked at you funny or said something that made it obvious. They hate you, because while everyone always says being different makes you special, your brand of different doesn't qualify. People tolerate you, but the fact is, you're disgusting. Hideous. The voice inside your head always confirms it. *You're worthless. You should die.*

It started when I was eleven. Someone gave me one of

those vanity mirrors with magnification. At first I was excited, playing with all the different settings—I could see the way I looked in the daylight or at night or in the office. It didn't take long before I saw past the soft glow of those lights on my cheeks and settled on something that was quite hideous.

I had pores.

Horrible, horrible black holes . . . all over my nose. Everyone else had to see those. Every single one of them screamed it in my brain: *Worthless.*

It's silly, when you think about it . . . that *pores*, something so small, could render everything else about a person worthless. But that's not the way the mind of someone with body dysmorphic disorder works. It's the fun-house mirror, constantly distorting and tangling reality and fantasy, making it impossible to see one from the other.

I spent hours staring at them in the mirror, squeezing them, making my face red and marked. I started wearing makeup to hide those giant pores. I didn't know anything about choosing the right color foundation for my face, so I'd go to school and people would ask me, "Why are you orange?" But it felt like armor, not shielding anything precious, but shielding *others* from having to see such horrors. Funny thing was, I didn't mind the orange as much as I minded what was underneath it—pores that likely no one could see but me.

Around that time I became aware of my nose, and, overnight, the pores took a back seat. Someone in my sixth-grade class made a comment about how you couldn't miss my beak of a nose if you tried, and suddenly the obsession that would haunt most of my teenage years was born. I had an Italian nose, a pronounced nose, one with a lot of "character," like my mother's and grandfather's. But what gave my mother and grandfather their character, what made my mother look beautiful and my grandfather look distinguished, somehow made me look like something that wasn't worth inhabiting space on this earth.

As the years went on, my nose only grew bigger. Or at least that's how I felt. I would never wear my hair in a ponytail and could only wear it loose, so that it hung over my face like a curtain. I fantasized every day about what it would be like to have a normal nose. I did those makeup shading techniques, which didn't help at all. I sat in front of the mirror for hours, covering the bump on my nose and wondering if I could take a file to the bone myself. I have about a hundred pictures of me from those years either taken head-on or with my hand covering my nose. In fact, I became so super aware of cameras that whenever one was nearby, my hand would automatically shield my face. I made jokes about the size of my nose to my classmates. I let people I knew call me Big Nose and the Schnoz and pretended to laugh along with them.

Truthfully, though, I wanted to die. I wrote my first suicide note at twelve. In it I gave away all my precious possessions to my family members. I tore it up when I realized that holding a pillow over my head wasn't going to work. I wrote more suicide letters, longer and longer ones, all of which lasted a few weeks or months in my drawer before I finally tossed them away. I stopped taking care of my appearance. Gradually I became more and more withdrawn so that even my parents couldn't deny something was wrong. I never told them about wanting to die, but whenever they asked me what was going on, I'd tell them I hated my nose. So my good, middle-class parents scraped their money together for a nose job.

I had the nose job the week I turned sixteen. My expectations were beyond unrealistic. Because I'd poured every second of my time into thinking about my horrible nose, I thought that once that problem was gone, all my worries would be gone too. For a while things were better. I started caring how I looked. Taking pictures was no longer a nightmare. People in school noticed and said I looked great.

But then that familiar voice started to creep its way in. *Worthless.*

Name a body part, and I had some sort of problem with it. Sometimes it was my thighs. My protruding belly. My boobs. I wanted to take a pair of scissors to all of it, at one time or another. Even, sad to say, my brand-new nose. I started thinking that it was "off," that it wasn't symmetrical, that my nostrils were too big. And those pores!

One problem fixed, my obsessive brain just went and found other things to obsess about. And I'm not Einstein, but I'm a smart person. I'd shake my head whenever I saw some plastic-surgery-obsessed celebrity who destroyed his or her face in the quest for perfection. So why didn't I realize then that it wasn't my looks but my *brain* that was the problem? No, instead I went from obsession to obsession, hating myself, wanting to hide myself away because I felt so worthless.

So what happened? Luckily, I didn't have the means, like some celebrities, to go under the knife again and again, or else I probably would've, and not gotten anywhere close to happy.

And no, I didn't have a grand epiphany that suddenly made me like myself. That's only for movies. In fact, it was a series of small realizations that happened over the course of many years. One was learning how distorted the reflection can be when I look at myself in the mirror. I remember thinking about how I still had a few pounds to lose, so I should probably skip lunch, when someone came up to me and said, "Oh my God, you're a walking skeleton." This happened so many times that I started to understand that something with the way my eyes perceived things was skewed. Your own eyes can lie.

One time someone told me I should start noting how often I said to myself, "You suck; you did that wrong; what's wrong with you?" That was when I learned how cruel I was—not to others, but to me. Not even my worst enemy would be so mean. I was my own harshest critic, and no one was judging my pants size or my nose or my pores more closely than myself. And not only that, the more I said those horrid things to myself, the more I fell into that rut of repeating that familiar *worthless* script, until I had no choice but to believe it. Your brain can be a real asshole sometimes.

Even now, with my teenage years so far behind me, sometimes I have to remind myself to shut my brain off, to tell it where to go. Sometimes I have to tear my eyes away from the mirror. Whenever I get depressed, it's usually because something has been marinating inside me for a while, and the asshole side of my brain has had its way with it. I have to make a conscious effort to switch the kind, nurturing part of my brain to the forefront. I make it tell myself nice things. I make it tell me to just live, do the day-to-day, take things as they come, and not dwell too much on my faults . . . not an easy task for a writer who is used to examining and over-thinking things. But hey—is it any wonder so many writers are depressed? They're sensitive, inside their own minds a lot, turning things over and trying to make sense of things. Sometimes I have to just *not* be a writer. To not analyze. To tune out shocking news headlines and celebrity gossip and politics and *CSI* and be blissfully ignorant to it all.

I've made peace with myself now. I'm never really pleased with what I see in the mirror. But I don't obsess (much). I don't dwell (much). I don't wake up at four anymore to get ready, and I don't tell myself I'm worthless.

You're not either. I promise.

How to Deal with Me . . . and My PTSD

by Melissa
Marr

I used to simply say I "didn't cope well" with the Bad Thing that had happened. Sometimes that's still the phrase I use. It's more comfortable than saying "Hi, I seem to be struggling with post-traumatic stress disorder." But let's just go for blunt here, okay?

Hi, I seem to be struggling with post-traumatic stress disorder. If we're going to be spending any time together, there are a few things you ought to know. It's totally okay if you don't want to deal with them—or me—but here's my "How To" if you choose to be around me.

First and foremost, I need to have my back to the wall in order to relax. Always. My house is organized that way. It's easy at home, but in public it gets complicated. In restaurants it can be an issue. I'm sorry if that means it takes longer to get seated. I'm extra sorry if I embarrass you by requesting a particular table or refusing one. The alternative is that there's a good chance I will need to walk out of the building suddenly.

Loud places make me flee too. I need to be able to hear anyone approaching me or mentioning me. It's not arrogance. I've been attacked in my home more than once. The first time was in high school, and the second time was in another home when I had roommates. Both times my attacker found out where I lived. Both times he talked to people, pointing me out, and I didn't hear either attacker asking about me. I didn't hear people telling him my name or where I lived. If I'd heard . . . maybe things would be different. For now, though, I need to be able to hear people. It's yet another aspect of something the therapists told me was "hypervigilance."

If it's *too* bright inside, I won't be comfortable. Bright means I'm exposed. It means I can be seen without realizing I'm being watched. I can't relax if we are too exposed. Even if it's dim, I always try to be alert. I scan the room; I take mental notes of where people are and what they're wearing. I suspect this is a benefit to me in writing. Characters' clothes are often outlined, as are the places they are standing and where they move. In reality, it's simply how I see the world. Details matter if we need to file a report later. Details matter if I'm to stand any chance of finding threats before they make me bleed. I sometimes hate that I think like that, but it's just a fact now.

Being close to me also means that we both sometimes agree that I will lie to you. I might tell you that of *course* I realize logically that I'm safe. Knowing the past doesn't mean it will repeat.

I mean, what are the odds, right? Except, well, it happened more than once. It's very hard to convince myself that there aren't other threats. I don't know that I could rebuild myself again. (Even as I say that, I know that what I mean is that I'm weary, and I don't know if I *want* to. I would. We both know that. I have kids. For them, I would find a way, but dear G-d, I am weary.)

I know you worry, too, and sometimes being the person dealing with my PTSD is extremely stressful. I get that, and I want to be easier for you, for my family, even for those who only encounter me casually. I want to be "normal" so desperately that sometimes I will choose to lie to you so you, at least, get a break from all of these rules I have to use in order to go out around people.

If I think you'll actually believe me, I will tell you that I'm doing well even when I'm not. I may even put my back to the room if I can force myself to do so in order to *prove* that I'm feeling confident. The truth, however, is that I will still find ways to check for security. Hypervigilance is the hardest part of PTSD. I have *tricks*. Life is about tricks and self-training to allow me to be among people and maintain the illusion of calm. Odds are that I've said that I always need to wash my hands before I eat. That's a safe excuse to locate the exits, to survey the crowd, to make sure I can stay. I will feel guilty that I have lied to you, even though it's because I *also* feel guilty that you worry, so I will wash my hands after I wander to the bathroom. Having PTSD means I have very clean hands.

If I can check the room, and if it's not too bright, and if

I can be tucked in with a wall to prevent people coming up behind me, we can relax and be like everyone else here . . . unless there is a sudden noise or someone touches me. Even when I try my best, I often startle to the point where we'll both be embarrassed. There are not as many tricks that work there.

Physical contact is simply frightening to me on a core level I cannot control. I initiate it in order to control it. I will hug you hello. I may kiss you hello. I establish a safe zone this way. I am in control. It lets me not be surprised by anyone reaching out. It lets me know you by your scent and height and the way you feel when you bump into me. Scent really helps. I like when you have a shampoo or lotion that is *you*. It becomes a sort of familiarizing trick that will help me know it's you and not startle as much if you reach out.

I hate the way my nervousness makes me jump away. It's not you who makes me jump or exclaim. It's the world. It's strangers. It's the fact that sudden, harmless brushes against me trigger reactions that I cannot always repress. I try, though, because I realize how difficult it is to have to deal with my responses to things that are not true threats. I hate embarrassing you.

I suspect you'll realize that there are places I simply fail at this, especially if I have to take a bus or train with you. I will offer to pay for a taxi or suggest we walk rather than be trapped in a box where there are so very many people to watch or corner me. They can see where we went and where we got on. They can track us.

221

Yes, I know it sounds paranoid. It might be . . . except that experience says it isn't. The man who attacked me in high school saw me, and he studied me. I didn't see him doing it. I was right *there* and still unaware. How do I know that there isn't another just like him? If I had done all of those things, followed the right rules, I might have been safe. I want to be safe. I want you to be safe too.

Despite all of that, the worries and the startling and the difficulties going out in public sometimes, I *want* to go out to dinner with you, especially when I am traveling. Going out helps me sleep when I travel. We can talk, and I'll have a drink or maybe two—not *many* drinks, of course. Alcohol slows reaction time. Talking, walking, and a drink or two will make me sleepy. I need that when I'm away from home. It keeps me from staying up all night with insomnia. It keeps me from dreaming sometimes too. If I'm lucky and I'm sleepy enough, it might even stop me from checking the doors, the windows, the locks, and, of course, looking under the bed and in the closet.

Okay, not *really*. If I'm in a room by myself and don't check for intruders, I won't be able to sleep. In truth, if I don't check more than once, I might not sleep or—worse yet—I will half wake in a night terror, reliving things that I would prefer to forget. Mostly I have dreams. I wake shaking, soaked in sweat, and unaware of where I am. They come in batches, so sometimes I travel with a nightlight. Seeing where I am when I wake helps.

Once in a great while, though, I have full-out night terrors.

Nothing helps with those. Night terrors suck. I know most of my triggers by now. In the past few years I've only had one night terror that was truly awful. My companion said I screamed for several minutes. Minutes. Actual *minutes*. I was caught reliving a Bad Thing, and no amount of trying to get me back to reality was working. I begged for my life. A witness saw me begging for my life.

Did I mention that sometimes PTSD is sort of embarrassing?

Overall, though, it's manageable. I won't ask you to stay overnight in my sleeping space, mostly because I fear you seeing that. I fear witnesses to what I'd rather forget. That was complicated when I was dating. It's complicated when people from out of town want to visit me.

I struggle to have guests in my home. Contractors are worse. Strangers—who are probably sweet and kind—frighten me simply because they are there. The Bad Thing happened in my home. It's made me mistrustful of allowing people to enter my space. If I invite you here, it's a huge statement of trust. Even so, guests are only allowed on the main floor. No one is to enter the floor where I sleep, where my children sleep. To add to my security, I have dogs—Rottweilers, to be precise. I have a security system. I have a handgun—and a lifetime of comfort with using one. All of these also make me seem a little paranoid. I accept that. Often, I laugh and smile and silently think that if you woke from sleep being assaulted you might feel just as paranoid, just as cautious. I don't want you to feel that type of worry, not ever.

Instead, I will tell you all of the ways it has gotten better. If I'm in a period of life with low stress, having these little traits is perfectly manageable most days. There are simple modifications on where I go, allowing extra time to check surroundings, and tactics to feel secure. Those are easy for me. If we get close, you'll adjust to them too. Some people require restaurant choices for certain diets. I require a few moments of extra security time.

When I'm at a higher stress level, it's . . . less manageable. I have insomnia and night terrors and cancel plans. I withdraw from anyone who knows me well enough to see the warning signs. My diagnosing therapist called it "unhealthy isolation" to allow me to "self-destruct."

Early on, it was much harder to deal. I didn't realize how frayed my edges were after the second assault until someone dropped a tray in the cafeteria where I was eating. That was the moment that I pinpoint as the realization that I wasn't "coping." I became so panicked that I wondered if that was what a heart attack felt like. It wasn't, obviously. It was a panic attack. I walked out, although I am told it was a near run.

Meals meant crowds. Crowds were dangerous, so I started skipping meals. Skipping meals meant hunger, so I supplemented my caffeine intake with a few amphetamines . . . which resulted in jitteriness and people asking *more* questions, which resulted in steadily withdrawing further from the people who loved me.

I ended up standing on a window ledge because it seemed

like it wouldn't get better. It seemed like I was weak. I *hate* feeling weak.

But time passes. It has passed, and I've learned these tricks to deal with my PTSD. Now we can sit in a restaurant where I couldn't even enter fifteen years ago. I can tell you about the events I've attended at my kids' schools. Sure, I went early or left early a few times, but I was *there*. I have learned rules that enable me to handle crowds. Sometimes I can even ride a subway or bus, and I have taught myself not to flinch as obviously when people touch me without warning.

After enough years finding ways to live with this, I can even talk about the ways that having PTSD has been an okay thing. I notice details about the world that I can harness for my job. I wrote this essay so that other people in my situation will know they aren't alone.

Silence doesn't help any of us. If we aren't afraid to say we have allergies or a cold or a broken arm, why should we be afraid to say we have something *else* medically out of the ordinary? The fact that you read as far as that last sentence, that you read this essay, that you picked up this anthology tells me that we can go out in public without apology on my part or worry on yours. It says that you won't think me impossible if I say not *this* restaurant or ask you to walk a few blocks or maybe switch seats with me so I can stay here and talk to you. It says we can find a way to deal with my PTSD.

Life by the Slice

by Wendy Toliver

I knew the best way to get my sixteen-year-old son, Chase[1], to break away from his busy summertime schedule of sleeping in and hanging out was to take him on a lunch date to the restaurant of his choice. We go with his second choice, because our favorite sushi place is closed on Mondays. We select a table on the patio overlooking the river and order pizzas—margherita for me and a custom one of pepperoni, spicy marinara, and olives for him. I pass him a napkin. It falls through the slats of the table, and we both giggle. As I pass him another napkin, this time placing it in his hand, I notice dry skin and what look like scratch marks on the back of his hand. I could offer him some lotion, but I already know he won't use it.

I told Chase what I wanted to talk about, and he agreed to put his own personal story out there in order to hopefully help

[1] The names in this essay have been changed.

people who are like him see they're not alone, and to help others better understand what he's going through.

He starts out explaining, "I'd say I have a mixture of anxiety, depression, and OCD. They sometimes go together, because if you have OCD, you roll stuff around in your mind over and over, and sometimes it gives you anxiety, and sometimes it makes you really depressed."

"Can you tell me about each of them?" I ask. "I don't want the Google definitions," I clarify, knowing he spends a lot of time on the Internet, trying to learn about himself and the world he lives in. "Tell me in your words."

As Chase's dark blue eyes shift to the upper right thoughtfully, I study my oldest son's face. He has a small pimple on his chin and a smattering of dark almost-whiskers on his upper lip. I've learned that I can use shaving as a point of negotiation, as in: *Yes, you can stay out an hour past your curfew, but only if you shave.* He knows it too, so he never does it on his own.

"When I have anxiety, my heart beats fast and my head sweats. I either can't sleep at all, or I feel like I need to sleep all of the time."

"What triggers it, do you think?" I ask.

"It's just everything. Anything. I can literally just think about having anxiety and either have a panic attack, or just sit there and hope it goes away. I have anxiety all the time, so I've gotten used to it. Really, panic attacks aren't as bad as the other stuff."

227

"Like the OCD and depression?"

"Yeah. The OCD sucks because you can't stop thinking about stuff, so it makes the depression and anxiety even worse. Like, when I want something, I can't stop thinking about it until I have it, then I can't stop thinking about something else. It never stops. And sometimes I get really depressed. I don't feel like myself. Hopeless. I don't want to do anything. I just try to continue. But sometimes it gets so bad I want to kill myself."

He's mentioned wanting to kill himself before. It's always been in the context of his dad or me telling him he can't do something like go to a particular rap concert, though. Hearing it in this milieu has much more of a graveness to it. "Why?" is all I can think of to ask at this point.

He shrugs and eats some pizza before answering. "Sometimes it just seems like the best option."

Though I try to keep my expression neutral, my eyes must be betraying the torrent of emotions I'm feeling, because he gives me a warm little smile, a flash of gold braces. "When I'm really depressed, it seems like a solid plan. Then I get scared that I'm going to kill myself. It's like my brain is going to kill me."

"Do you ever ask for help?" I ask, wondering how in the world I could have missed something like this. I feel like my sons and I—and their friends for that matter—have very open relationships. I make an effort to provide a nonjudgmental environment for all of them and try to help them feel comfortable talking to me about anything, no matter how tough the subject. Selfishly I want to be the one he comes to, but if not me, I hope he has a friend, a friend's parent, his school counselor—someone—he reaches out to when he feels so hopeless.

"Not really. I know I just need to get through it."

"What about when you saw Dr. Alan? Did that help?" When Chase was in the fourth grade, his dad and I noticed some behaviors that concerned us. Chase would wash his hands so often, and in such scalding water and with such strong soaps, that his hands became red and scaly. In time his skin flaked and rubbed off, and sometimes it even bled. Though I replaced all the hand soaps with gentle, moisturizing formulas and made lotion readily available, his hands looked like they'd been badly burned.

He took multiple showers a day, too. It started out with two or three, and I remember thinking, *All moms should be so lucky to have such a clean kid*. One night I'd made pizza for his friend and him, and after Chase ate a slice, he disappeared upstairs. I suspected he couldn't wipe the grease off his hands well enough, so he'd gone to wash them in his bathroom sink. However, he was taking a shower. Soon he was taking up to seven showers in a single day.

Whenever his dad or I noticed him going upstairs for a shower, we reminded him that he'd recently taken one. Still, he insisted on showering again and again, sometimes sneaking them when he thought we wouldn't notice. When I asked him to use towels more than once before throwing them in the laundry hamper, he began hiding the once-used towels in his room. Chase's showering and handwashing were getting in the way of "normal" ten-year-old life, so I made him an appointment with a child psychologist. Though not an official diagnosis, Dr. Alan said Chase had "OCD tendencies."

"Dr. Alan was nice and everything, but my mind was so screwed up, I barely even remember talking to him," Chase answers.

"When do you feel like your mind got so screwed up?" I ask.

He wipes a strand of hair off his cheek. His thick, auburn mane flows out of his flat-brimmed cap well past his shoulders in soft waves. Earlier that day an older lady stopped him to say, "It's always the boys who get the most beautiful hair." He's wearing a nice T-shirt, chino-style shorts, and leather flip-flops. He wears nice clothes these days—but that wasn't always the case. "Fourth grade, probably," he says.

I nod, unsurprised. That was a tough year. In addition to the handwashing and showers, when he went to school, he wore clothes that were too small or perhaps had stains or holes in them. He had plenty of nice clothes in his closet, and I couldn't figure out why he insisted on wearing the ones I kept bagging up to donate. The backpack I bought him for school remained hanging in his closet, unused, in favor of taking his books to school in a plastic grocery sack. When his dad or I asked him why he wouldn't wear his nice clothes or take his backpack to school, he said, "I don't want them to get dirty."

The minute he got off the bus in the afternoons, he'd sprint to the bathroom, where he'd relieve himself—as he never went to the bathroom at school—and then wash his hands, shower, and put on a different set of old clothes.

His dad and I asked him about school, friends, body issues—anything we could think of that might be causing him stress. According to Chase, everything was just fine. No one bullied him; his teachers (he had two homeroom teachers who job-shared) were okay. Then, after he'd been going to Dr. Alan and his school counselor for a couple of months, he told us some concerning stories about one of his teachers, Mrs. Green. For example, when he was done with his math work and decided to read his library book, she threw his book against the wall. Another day, she made him stand up against a wall (facing outward) because he wouldn't stop clicking his pen. It sounded too cruel—and, frankly, suspicious—to be true. But when I called a couple of his classmates, their stories aligned with Chase's. His dad and I soon realized the times he took the most showers and was the most "fidgety" (tapping pens, bouncing foot, shaking hands, cracking knuckles) correlated with the days Mrs. Green was his homeroom teacher.

I felt a pressing need to meet with his teachers, especially Mrs. Green, so I called to make an appointment. No one called back. I e-mailed. No one wrote back. I called the school secretary to try to get through that way. No call back. I dropped in during scheduled teacher planning, but Mrs.

Green was meeting with the other fourth-grade teachers and wouldn't talk to me. Finally, I got ahold of the principal and arranged a meeting with him, the school counselor, and both of Chase's teachers, with Dr. Alan on standby.

The meeting got us nowhere. Mrs. Green did not come (I still don't know why she wasn't there, because she'd previously agreed to it), the principal merely stuck his head in, and Ms. Holmes did a lot of shrugging and said if the things Chase had accused Mrs. Green of doing were true, she was sure she'd had good reason.

The sudden resurgence of guilt makes it difficult to swallow my bite of pizza. I've never forgiven myself for letting it go so easily. I should have insisted upon another meeting. I shouldn't have succumbed to my husband's reasoning that the school year was almost over. I should have told Mrs. Green how hard a time my son was having when it was her days to teach. When his teachers turned down my offer to volunteer in the classroom, I should have volunteered at the school in general, so I could be there. "Mrs. Green was terrible," I say, breaking out of my neutral-reporter stance. "I'm so sorry I didn't do more to get you out of her class, Chase."

"She wasn't *that* bad," he says. "Really. It was embarrassing how you kept wanting to talk to her. If you really want to know what bothered me so much, it was you and Dad, always nagging me about grades."

I struggle to keep my forehead from wrinkling. "You had

good grades in the fourth grade," I say. And then I remember. One of his grades wasn't.

While we had Ms. Holmes and the school counselor in the school meeting room, Chase's dad and I asked about an F he'd received in English. When Ms. Holmes showed us the grade book, it was evident that they'd only been given one project, and he'd received a low score because he'd written something other than what had been assigned. As a writer myself, I considered it "thinking outside of the box," and shrugged it off. Especially since, as recommended by his school counselor, the district had had Chase tested, and at ten, he'd scored around a sixteen- or eighteen-year-old intelligence level. Not that we needed a test to tell us he was smart.

"Do you think you're smart?" I ask, still reeling from the idea that Chase had felt so much pressure from his dad and me for grades, even six years ago.

Chase nods. "Yeah. But I don't think school is worth having mental issues."

"When were your 'mental issues' the worst, do you think?" I ask, trying to put together some kind of timeline.

"Fourth, sixth, all of junior high . . ."

I was not surprised in the least that he deliberately didn't mention fifth grade, because Dr. Alan had recommended Zoloft (an antidepressant that helps people with depression, panic, anxiety, and obsessive-compulsive symptoms) and it had almost immediate results with Chase's showering, hand washing, and tics. Also, his teacher, Mrs. Hemsworth, made a world of difference for Chase in the wake of a tumultuous fourth grade. She went out of her way to make our son feel accepted, loved, and free to leave the classroom if need be. Shortly after starting her class, he was able to wean off Zoloft and his therapy sessions.

For the sixth grade and junior high, his report cards were mainly Bs and Cs. When Chase was in junior high, he waited until the last possible hour to turn everything in. His dad and I pestered him, because we hated not knowing if he was going to get a 4.0 or a 2.0 until the report card was posted. "You could get straight As if you'd only ____" was something we said often, filling in the blank with "turn in your home-work," "be more respectful to your teachers," or "try." We had several meetings with his school counselor and tried to keep on top of him, especially when it came to turning in the assignments he'd done. His mantra during this time was: *This is junior high. The grades don't matter.* But now that he was in high school, where the grades certainly did matter, they were worse than ever.

"Not high school?" I ask, wondering if he meant to leave it off.

"Not too much."

"So why'd you end your sophomore year with three Fs?"

"Because I didn't go to school."

His dad and I went on an out-of-country vacation, and upon our return we were shocked to discover he hadn't been to the majority of his classes for eleven days. Sometimes he'd been marked "truant," which meant he'd been in the building but hadn't gone to class. Since they were unexcused absences, the schoolwork and tests or quizzes given on those days could not be made up. One of those days he'd gone in to the counselor because he was having a panic attack, and my mother, who was taking care of him while his dad and I were away, took him to the doctor and began the process of determining why he was having so many panic attacks.

"What were you doing instead of going to school?" When I asked the question before, he told me he'd gone to a movie or shopping at Hastings, but there had to be more if it was eleven days' worth of absences. I made him take a drug test. He was clean.

"Sleeping at my friend Kacey's house on the floor," he answers, giving me something new this time.

"So you'd wake up at six something, drive down to school, and go to his house to sleep? And then come home after school, so my mom wouldn't suspect anything?"

"Yeah."

Once I got home from vacation, we had another appointment with Chase's doctor. Packets were mailed to his school, and various teachers filled them out for us. In the end, the doctor prescribed Zoloft, the drug Chase had successfully taken six years earlier.

"But you don't feel like sophomore year was bad, mental health–wise?"

"No. I kind of dug myself in a hole by missing so much

school, but I can still graduate. It's not that hard, so I shouldn't get stressed about it." He made up his failed classes in a couple of weeks earlier this summer. He can play the game; he just doesn't play by the same rules as most kids. He never has. I have to keep reminding myself of this. "Besides, the older I get, the more I am used to the way I am."

"What would you tell someone who is going through a similar experience with mental illness?" I ask.

"Some of the things I do to help are watch TV, take baths, listen to music, and go on a drive. Also, don't be afraid to go to the doctor or a psychologist or whatever. Zoloft has helped me a lot." He's been taking a low dose for about three months now. As his mom, I can add that having some semblance of a routine and letting him know plans as early as possible are helpful too.

"Are you happy?" I ask, again slipping out of my neutral-reporter persona to become the mom who wants this for her son most of all.

He stops eating and looks me in the eyes. "Yeah."

I eat some more of my lunch and let this sink in. Despite all of this—the stress, anxiety, panic attacks, nagging parents, feeling like his brain is going to kill him—Chase is happy. He has quite a few friends. They love hanging out with him and think he's hilarious. Even though he ditched much of his last semester of school, his teachers and counselor seem to like him. He has no desire to look at other schools. Yesterday a friend's dad told me he's glad our sons are friends, and a couple of weeks before another friend's mom told me how they enjoyed having him on their family vacation, and how happy he is.

As we box up my leftover pizza (he ate all of his), I thank Chase for his time, knowing that he's antsy to get home and hang out with friends. Our conversation shifts to tomorrow's big event: getting his wisdom teeth out. He's already researched what to expect before, during, and after the operation.

"It's going to be fine," I say, just as much to myself as to him.

All of it.

I'm a Survivor

by Cindy L. Rodriguez

When I was twenty-three years old, I left Connecticut for Boston for what should have been an amazing experience. I had recently been hired to be a researcher for the *Boston Globe*'s award-winning investigative team, a dream come true for a young journalist. Over the next two years, however, depression slowly ruined me, although many people close to me never knew.

When I tried to fight through the depression myself, I wrote in my journal.

Years later, when my mind was clear enough to make sense of what had happened and was happening to me, I wrote an article about it for the *Hartford Courant*.

Many years after that, when I decided to write a young adult novel, the central topic was depression.

Words have always been key to my understanding of others, myself, the world. What a powerful thing—when words become stories and stories provide windows and mirrors for readers. But the truth is that I never saw myself—a Latina with depression—in the stories I read. This, plus the general social stigma against mental illness, plus the added cultural stigma of not wanting to be *la loca de la familia* caused me to endure worsening symptoms and persist with my normal routine for far too long. While endurance and persistence can be admirable traits, in this context they created a damaging emotional and psychological resistance that prevented me from seeking help.

Writing about depression—in my journal, in the *Hartford Courant*, in *When Reason Breaks*—helped me, yes, but now, after years of managing the disease, I am more keenly aware that I write and talk about depression, especially about Latinxs with depression, because it's still something we in the Latinx community don't openly talk about. We lack the words, the stories, the mirrors, and this is harmful, perhaps even deadly, considering the statistics.

I am one of those statistics.

I survived it.

You can too.

I have learned to manage it.

You can too.

There is always hope.

I truly believe that, which is why I share my story.

It was a rainy February night in 1997 when it became apparent that the depression was no longer a temporary emotion but a disease that had invaded every part of my life. I had gotten into my car after work and cried all the way home. I can't remember why. But I remember feeling like I was choking, like every nerve in my body was numb, like someone was squeezing my heart, and everything good inside of me had been twisted around. I remember feeling hopeless. I remember wanting to disappear.

I never considered cutting myself or committing suicide, but I contemplated other plans that would remove me from my situation. Like getting into my car and driving far away to anywhere. Like joining the Peace Corps and asking to be stationed in the most remote area in the world. I knew, deep down, that moving someplace new would not solve my problem, but I ached with a need to escape. At times I thought about getting into an accident, like driving my car into a tree, not hard enough to kill myself, but hard enough to land me in a hospital, where, maybe, someone would see what was really wrong and I'd get help without actually asking for it.

Because I didn't know how to ask for help, and, at times, didn't think I could or should. Because I was raised by smart, strong people who fought for what we had, who pushed forward even when it was painful and risky. Because I thought asking for help might be a sign of weakness, and doctors are for when you're bleeding or something is broken.

But that February night I realized that I *was* bleeding and broken, that I'd risk everything if I continued to simply push ahead, that asking for help was the strongest, smartest, bravest thing I could do. I knew then that this thing eating away at me would not just go away. For a long time I was convinced it would. I believed that the traits I had inherited from those before me, like frankness and humor, would overpower this flaw.

But days and months had blurred into more than a year. Fatigue had seeped into my bones, and smiling became an effort—a false statement. I was tired all day and couldn't sleep at night. I called in to work sick with a flu I didn't have. I forced myself out of bed to make it in other days. My memory was deteriorating. I could listen to someone talk at length and not absorb a single word. I have no detailed recollection of certain events.

Still, I thought the depression was situational. I was having a rough time at work, feeling beat-up emotionally and unappreciated. With my career being such a significant part of my identity, I felt shaken and unsure of my talents and abilities. Something inside me was fighting back. I thought I could pull myself out of it.

That February night my mom convinced me that this was bigger. That it was something I may have inherited. She told me how she had struggled to raise the three of us—me, my sister, and my brother, only five years separating the oldest from the youngest. She told me how she'd spend whole days in bed after we went to school but got up and pushed forward when the school day was over and we came home.

She told me about my grandmother, who raised five

children as a single parent after her husband, my mom's dad, died at the age of forty. How she was mostly stoic and serious, rarely giggly or snuggly with her children. How, at one point, she got into the habit of sleeping with her arms crossed over her chest so that it would be easy for a family member to remove her body from the house if she died in the night.

This was out of my control, my mom said that night. She knew because she had seen it before and had experienced it herself. "You are definitely depressed," she said. "Promise me you'll see someone." Okay . . . but what then? Even though I was an educated woman with a great job that provided health insurance, I still didn't see myself on a therapist's couch. Maybe because my grandmother never treated her depression. Maybe because my mother took medication but refused to see a psychiatrist. Maybe because as well-read as I was, I never saw a Latina character being traditionally treated for mental illness.

Nonetheless, I went. Six days later I sat in a psychiatrist's office, unsure of what to do exactly. Wasn't this a luxury for wealthy people? Or a necessity for people with real problems, like battered women? It was hard to justify needing this, being an otherwise perfectly healthy and successful twenty-five-year-old. Yet, when I opened my mouth, a load of hurt poured out, and the hour flew by.

Ten years later I was planning and drafting what would become *When Reason Breaks*, my debut young adult novel about depression, attempted suicide, and the life and work of Emily Dickinson. While writing, I knew some readers would wonder why either of the two main characters—Emily Delgado and Elizabeth Davis—would want to kill herself. Nothing tragic happened to either of them. To some readers, none of their problems will be seen as good enough reasons to attempt suicide. They'll want a big reveal moment: "Oh, she was (fill in the blank with a horrible experience). No wonder she's depressed and suicidal. That's a legitimate reason."

When I was seriously, clinically depressed, I didn't think I had a right to be because, like my characters, nothing tragic had happened to me. I wanted to have a significant event, something I could point to and say, "Aha, that's the reason. If I address this one, obvious, horrible thing that happened to me, then I'll be okay." But I didn't have that thing. Many depressed people don't. And with the absence of something obviously wrong in my life, I pushed through the days, thinking what some people might think about my characters: My problems weren't significant enough.

This kind of thinking can lead to tragedy because the depression goes untreated, which happens too often in general and, specifically, in the Latinx community.

National health organizations report that Latinxs are at higher risk for depression than other minorities. Women experience major depression more often than men, and of students in grades nine through twelve, significantly more Latinas have attempted suicide than their non-Latina peers. Yet, most Latinxs with mental health problems never get treated. A lack of access to affordable services and the stigma attached to mental illnesses are cited as barriers to treatment. Untreated depression can lead to suicide, which is the third leading cause of death for all people aged fifteen to twenty-four.

Studies show that Latinxs often complain to doctors about individual symptoms of depression, such as physical pain or an inability to sleep, and are, therefore, treated for those specific complaints. Meanwhile, a diagnosis of depression is delayed or never determined. My resistance to treatment came in the form of denial or perhaps stubbornness. I knew something was wrong with me. I had all of the telltale signs. Still, I put off contacting my primary care doctor, who then referred me to a psychiatrist. I kept thinking, or hoping, that if I did something different, like exercise more, everything else would change.

These statistics and my own experience with depression got me thinking about how it's represented in young adult fiction, and I realized that in the books I've read, white characters are more likely to sit on a psychiatrist's couch. Most of the Latinx characters in novels I've read fight through mild to severe depression without medical help, or they are somehow detained, in a treatment facility or group home, and the therapy is required.

These narratives do represent what's happening, in general, in Latinx communities, according to the research, but if we never see Latinx characters seek and receive traditional therapy, I fear we are sending the message that comprehensive therapy for depression is, indeed, reserved for wealthy white people. While many Latinxs do not seek treatment, some do, and we need to hear those individual stories in addition to the overall statistics linked to Latinx communities.

Moving beyond statistics of an entire community and looking at individual stories can also help writers avoid the creation of "a single story." In her 2009 TED Talk, novelist Chimamanda Ngozi Adichie explains "the danger of a single story," which occurs when the mainstream media and other dominant power structures present an entire community as a single, definitive story illustrated with a handful of images. She relays her experiences as a Nigerian encountering people, including her college roommate, who had fixed ideas about all Africans based on their limited exposure to stories from the continent. She says if you show a people as one thing over and over again, that is what they become. One story becomes the only story, and this only serves to emphasize how we are different rather than how we are similar.

She even admits she employed the single-story mentality in relation to immigration, which is portrayed as synonymous with Mexicans. When she visited Guadalajara, she said she felt ashamed to realize she was observing Mexicans through the lens of the single immigration story presented in the news. "Stories matter. Many stories matter," she says. That she first wrote white characters who ate apples and talked about the weather, instead of creating Nigerian characters, is an example of "how impressionable and vulnerable we are in the face of a story, particularly as children."

I fear the single story when it comes to the portrayal of Latinxs with mental health issues. Latinx characters with depression, anxiety, or other mental illnesses are most often portrayed as resilient and capable of carrying on without seeking medical attention. We inadvertently support mental health stigmas by creating Latinx characters who ignore or push through obvious symptoms and never get professional help. If we ignore the Latinxs seeking help for mental illnesses by not representing them in stories, we are essentially presenting a single story. We are saying "This is the Latinx reality," and we do not even hint at other possibilities.

The dominant message in "mirror books" for young Latinxs with mental health issues seems to be "soldier on." Characters like them do not seek treatment. If we want young Latinx readers to consider traditional treatment for mental illnesses—if we want to avoid the danger of a single story—then we have to more often portray this in fiction.

In *When Reason Breaks*, one of the main characters visits a doctor and gets medication but doesn't take it. Later, however, the character accepts real help after her suicide attempt. She commits herself to traditional therapy, which includes medication, counseling, and a safety plan. The story includes some of the resistance cited in medical research, but this resistance is not admirable and leads nowhere good. I did not want to create a depressed character who could just "get over it" through willpower, positive thinking, or a personal or romantic relationship. It was important for me to show that the only way she would get better was through a combination of medication, therapy, and a commitment to better understand herself and the disease.

I hope that as the Latinx population continues to grow, barriers are removed so that more Latinxs seek treatment for mental illnesses. I also hope more children's authors tackle the variety of mental illnesses and show characters of color getting help at some point instead of suffering through their pain. Francisco X. Stork's beautiful novel, *The Memory of Light*, is a good example, as it features a Latina protagonist and centers on recovery. Maybe more teens will see themselves in these books and understand what took me a long time to figure out: Your problems are significant enough. You don't need a "real reason" to feel the way you do. Depression *is* the real reason, and you have greater chances of surviving and managing it if you get professional help.

Anxiety, the Weed

by Candace Ganger

It started early.

In the middle of class, after my first-grade teacher said I couldn't go to the bathroom, I urinated all over myself. I couldn't hold it; I tried. Immediately I was so embarrassed, my world faded to black. As if there were chains around my wrists and ankles, a mass of fear coiled snug around my body like a python. I gasped and clawed hard at my throat for air. But the more I panicked, the harder the pulses pushed into me. I couldn't run, couldn't move. With everyone's eyes hard-pressed on me, I just sat there, becoming part of that wet, cold-tiled floor forever. If I close my eyes, I still see the sad outline of me there, dying inside. And those same feelings of worry and fear still live inside me like a plague. For different reasons now, sure. But always waiting for the right moment to resurface. I could be at a party, surrounded by friends, in line at the coffee shop, or all alone with no stressor in sight.

An anxiety attack to me is a mental prison holding my thoughts and body captive. There is no escape or refuge when it happens. My heart jackhammers, my lungs deflate, and I lose all control over my limbs, thoughts, and, mostly, perception of reality. I become the villain in my own story, not fighting the world, but fighting myself, and the only cause of my undoing is me.

At first glance I appear as any other. I'm a mother, a writer, a runner. I may be out crossing off an errand list or grabbing dinner from a drive-through with my family. You might pass me doing laps in the cemetery or see me getting my daily latte fix at the coffee shop that's come to know my order before I step inside the door. To the outside world I seem "fine." I look "normal," whatever that means. But on the inside, I'm in a million broken pieces.

The anxiety begins with a vague, prickling sensation like a tight hug that won't let up until I'm dizzy. It makes no prejudice on where I am or who I'm with at the time and doesn't care how hard I fight it. Those small, tingling waves slosh together until my blood swells and circles like a riptide. Muscles tense from head to toe, and all I hear is a scream from somewhere deep inside me, roaring to get free. These feelings can be a slow trickle or all at once like a spark. There might be a lead-up, or trigger, or there may be nothing at all. To those who've never experienced an anxiety attack, all of this may seem strange or like my behavior changes out of nowhere. *What's wrong with me?* I wrestle. But it always begins somewhere. And some days everything is a trigger.

Every. Thing.

The traffic. The hum of mufflers in traffic. The smoke from the cars. The sun. It will burst someday. Today could be that day. It's too bright, too warm. Or maybe the sun is hidden because a storm is coming. The kind that could rip through town and destroy everything. Those clouds are too dark, the sky, too ominous. It could be the swarms of people. Everywhere I go, there they are. The proximity of the people. They're too close. *Everything* is too close. I'm shrinking into nothing while they freely move around me without chains binding them. I am trapped. There is no way out. NO. WAY. OUT.

Anxiety is a poisonous seed—a weed. It's not something I *want* in my garden. All of this stress might have started with that classroom incident all those years ago, or maybe it morphed from the bullying thereafter. It could've been my parents' tumultuous divorce or maybe being so overweight that I never felt at home in my own olive skin. It might have been the traumatizing loss I suffered in the years of puberty when I desperately wanted to find my place in the world and struggled so hard to do so. It could've been none of these things or all of them smashed together into one cancerous mass. The starting point doesn't matter. One by one, weed by weed, all the fear and worry and wasted time and energy grew and grew until weeds overtook my beautiful garden, my soul. Until I felt ugly inside. Sometimes, dead inside. And other times, nothing at all.

The weeds, however long I panic over them, never bloom into anything pretty or logical. I *know* this—but even still. I give in, not because I *can't* fight, but because at times I don't know how. Anxiety looks for cracks, weakness in my foundation and anything that makes me human. Its only job is to manipulate everything I believe about myself and the world around me until I can't tell what's wrong or right or anything in between. I've lost countless hours in the black of night feeding this beast, knowing full well nothing good can come from all the worry. Knowing all I'm doing is fading a little bit more each time. And then, for good measure, I worry about that, too.

Anxiety doesn't give a damn. Not even a little.

When I'm curled in ball with insomnia or fighting the urge to sprint out of a crowded room, the anxiety whispers all the lies into my ear. Until my thoughts are not mine. They belong to anxiety now. My world of mostly normal fears (clowns, farm machinery, mirrors—the usual) magnifies into something too big to conquer. It's utterly exhausting to live this way, and, with no end in sight, the cycle repeats again and again. But I didn't know how to fix it, how to fix me. I only knew one of us had to go—me or the anxiety.

After a lifetime of fighting the stress, the day eventually came when I couldn't do it by myself anymore. It wasn't just one moment but a series of them that brought me to this place. When I hear about defeat, I think of that feeling, knowing this disorder had been killing me from the inside out. It happened so gradually, I didn't even realize how much of me the stress had stolen. Was I even capable of happiness anymore? I honestly wasn't so sure. I wanted to hide, disappear. There had been times, I remember, when I emerged as the social butterfly (mostly in and out of high school, when I could ignore some of the fears) but sometime after that, it dissolved, and even if happiness had resurfaced here and there, I was mostly pretending so no one would know about my secret poison. I only wanted to be as free as everyone else seemed to be.

I stopped leaving the house, avoided people at all costs, and at my low point fell into such a depression that other weeds in my garden (OCD and anorexia) had reared their ugly heads. It felt like all my flaws had ganged up against me. I remember looking around at all the positives in my life—a loving husband, two wonderful children, my health, and countless other things—and my brain only wanted to ruin every piece. My stopping point, somewhere along the way, was in seeing how my children look to me as a steadfast support system, a hero. They can*not* grow up believing this is the only way to be. I knew I couldn't continue living like this because, honestly, it's not living; it's suffering silently.

During that time, which was a few years back, I took a long, hard look at my life and realized some very important things. The anxiety is *not* my fault. I *can't* will myself to control it without the proper tools and/or medication. I *can* conquer it. And most of all, I am *not* less of a person for having this battle. The truth is that everyone has anxiety. Some are just better at managing this weed than others, and I was *not* one of those

people. So maybe no one is "normal" or "okay," and that realization gave me hope.

The first step for me was an obvious one but not necessarily the easiest—picking up the phone. The anxiety in holding
the receiver to my ear proved how very much I needed to seek
treatment. It took some digging to find the right path, but after
some serious reflection, I went to therapy—three separate
therapists, actually, because I'm a "go big or go home" kind of
gal (which, ironically, may have contributed to my anxiety to
begin with).

Therapist number one was a small-boned woman with
holes in her stockings but warmth in her wisdom. There sat
seven lamps, four chairs, and more than twenty board games
stacked on a tall, wooden bookshelf. I counted these things
every time because the familiarity gave me comfort. After a
few sessions she noticed an anxiety-driven tic—rubbing my
knuckles together until bloody—and gifted me a small, marbled
stone with an indentation meant for my thumb. It's known as
a "worry stone," and though it took some practice, it keeps the
stress at bay when my fingers are fumbling for friction.

Over the weeks there I learned how to visualize a calming scenario, coupled with breathing exercises to help put the
stress at bay before a major panic onset. For me there is no
calmer place than the ocean—the Atlantic, Cocoa Beach. The
sound of crashing waves, wind in my hair, and warm, lem-
ony sun on my skin (that will not burst into flames) bring me
closer to breathing. Breathing is not easy in a panic, and it

took a lot of practice to learn *how* to breathe when my throat closes up. I wouldn't have known this if I hadn't made those appointments I put off for so long.

We charted a map of my fears, so visually I had a frame of reference. Surprisingly, there's a big difference between "I have nothing to wear," "there are too many people in the room," and "someone died." What I took from this is that anxiety doesn't care where my fears fall on the scale. A one is the same as a ten in my tangled mess of perception, and *all* thoughts will leave me paralyzed. But at least I could see the things I worried about and the effect they had on my mental state at any given time. Meaning, if I can spot the trigger, acknowledge it, and rely on the tools I practiced, I might have a chance at bypassing the attack. Knowledge really is power. Anxiety thought it could hide from me for so long; it's empowering to now be the predator, seeking all that darkness to force into light and deal with it head-on.

I know now there really is no other way.

The second professional I went to specialized in something called cognitive behavioral therapy, or CBT. This woman, whose wall clock ticked and tocked me into a new form of insanity, gave me the tools I needed to be "present." So much of my life had been hiding or distraction in order to avoid anxiety. By putting the phone away and immersing myself in my children's laughter, or focusing on the meal I cooked for my family, my senses came alive in a whole new way. I realized how much I'd missed amid all my worrying.

Jokes. Moments. All the warm and fuzzy feelings that disappeared if not caught as they happened. This is why I'd felt so empty—because the anxiety stripped away my ability to enjoy anything at all.

I won't lie. This type of therapy still takes A LOT of practice, dedication, and the ability to push through the discomfort. It's not something I noticed changing right away, and at times I only frustrated myself in not being present every moment of every day. It's a lifelong cycle I want to break, so of course it can't be fixed overnight. Now when I find myself hiding from how I feel, I refocus my energy the best I can. Sometimes I succeed. Sometimes I fail. But at least now I try.

I couldn't tell you when my thinking began to change. It wasn't a particular day but maybe a string of instances. As I sat on the floor with my son, I heard him—like *really* heard him—in a way I never had before. His eyes appeared more aquatic, and his little hands seared into my memory as they sat in mine. I saw my past and how much time I'd lost. I looked to my future and decided anxiety couldn't steal another second. And I soaked up the *now* for the beautiful gift it is. I am not owed any amount of time on this earth, and one day I will pass. I looked at my son and thought, *How do I want to spend my time here—stressing out over every little thing or enjoying it?*

During another powerful attempt at bettering my mind, I joined an anonymous support group. Well beyond my comfort zone, I found in others what I'd been lacking: acceptance, like the old Serenity Prayer. To my right sat a mother who'd lost her son. To my left, an elderly widower who still carried his beloved wife's picture in his pocket. The circle of trust taught me anxiety comes in many forms, for many reasons. My circumstances made me think back to the first therapist and the anxiety scale. While compared to those dealing with tragic loss, whose anxiety may be at a ten, mine may only seem to be a five. But in that room, embraced by so many strangers who understood the rooted pain, the numbers didn't matter.

Anxiety is blind.

You can be the richest tycoon in the world or live in a slum; you can be the most popular friend in your circle or have no friends at all. You may have suffered a hundred horrible losses or none. Anxiety knows no bounds, and a one to one person could be a ten to someone else, so have compassion for those around you. Most times you won't even know someone is fighting this demon until you ask. Or, in my case, see me at a support group, find my thumb in a worry stone, or watch me silently unravel in line at the grocery store.

If anxiety eats at your brain the way it does mine, I want you to know you are *not* alone. It may feel like it when the tornado stampedes your body and thoughts. You may think everyone is looking at you, talking about you. That you're weird or different or something's wrong with you. You may wonder if it will ever stop, if the list of potential catastrophes has an end point. You may even fear you'll never regain control of your hijacked mind again. Anxiety wants you to believe this, because if you don't, you take away the power.

This is the seed planted. *This* is the lie.

For the longest time I let this disorder disrupt my life. My identity became wrapped up in this weed. If I'm not the worrier, the cautious, the high-strung negotiator who cares too much about everything, who the hell am I? I'll tell you who I am. I'm a mother, wife, writer, runner, obnoxious cat lover, and obsessive latte drinker but *not* my anxiety. And you are *not* yours.

And though I'm far better off than never getting help at all, there are still times I feel the panic rushing in before I can breathe or visualize. I am imperfect, searching for a better way of living, and in that comes trial and error. Some medications aren't right for me. Some therapies have failed. Because anxiety is THAT STRONG.

But that doesn't mean we should stop trying to fight it.

When I step foot outside my house into a place unknown, if my lungs tighten and sizzle, or if my heart speeds, I try to remember who's in control. I will not always succeed. There are many times I've had to cower into a ball and let the tears soak the floor. I'm only human, and, honestly, being human is just plain hard at times. Life will ebb and flow. It will always bring a strange mix of good and bad or high and low. But every day is a new day to take control back. To pull all that darkness from your bones, rest it in the palm of your hand, close your eyes, and blow until all that's left are wisps of air and something you may have missed all this time—serenity, calm, peace, and acceptance of who you are and the beauty you're made of.

I know the anxiety will always be there in some little pocket of me, waiting to emerge when I'm weak. But in knowing this, I've already taken back some of the power. As I struggle to regain control of this story—*my* story—I now know how to edit the rough draft of who I've become (via therapeutic tools), how to rewrite the ending (with hope), and which villain to kill off (anxiety). When I say it like that, all the anxiety that's colored my world shrinks to something manageable, something not so scary. I can stop thinking about all the ways I'm dying or will die, and all the ways something might go wrong or hurt me or scare me or haunt me or make me uncomfortable. The only focus now is living a life without fear or shame . . . for being me.

And all my hope for you, my friends, is the very same.

And so much more.

xoxo

By Any Means Necessary

by Sara Zarr

Most days are like this:

I wake up. Before I get out of bed, I have a certain amount of worry over how the day will go. Will I get up, drink coffee, eat breakfast, feel pretty good, maybe go for a walk, do some writing, see a friend? Will I get through my to-do list? Will I be scared or anxious or lonely? Will I spend too much time on Twitter? Will my relationship with food go okay? Will I stare in the mirror too long, judging my face, my shape, my weight?

These questions don't drag me down. They're just questions; they're only thoughts. And it's normal for me to struggle with all of those thoughts, along with things like not knowing how to relax, spending half my day deciding what I should do and how I should structure my time, what I should eat, whom I should see.

But I'm used to that part of being me. At most, the questions make me uneasy, and I still get up and do routine things:

259

coffee, breakfast, walk, sit at my desk, tinker with my work, fiddle with my to-dos. The day is either good or it's meh or kinda sucky, but that's fine, just fine.

Other days are like this:

Sometime between getting out of bed and standing in front of the coffeepot, I feel the cloud. Or not a cloud, exactly, because it's as much in me as over me. It's a mass of negative thoughts. Maybe more like quicksand than a cloud. Something's dragging on me; something's pulling me.

I feel fear and worthlessness, or fear that I'm worthless.

Before I even have my breakfast, I'm already plagued by the certainty that I'll always be this, I'll never be that, I'm doomed, I'm messed up, I'm broken, I'm all alone in the universe. That part—the loneliness—is both crushing and strange. Crushing because it feels like the absolute and final truth about me. Strange because I do have friends. I'm happily married. I have interesting people in my life whom I know through my work as a writer and through church and through the neighborhood. Evidence suggests that I have a certain place in the world, and there are no legit reasons to feel doomed, broken, alone.

My quicksand mind says, *No, the evidence lies.*

The *real* truth is that my friends don't really know me, my husband has never understood me, and no one truly grasps how lazy and terrible and mean I am. Everyone has fallen for an act. Except *some* people probably see through it and can tell that I'm alone and don't know how to be a friend, don't know how to be normal, don't know how to be healthy, don't know how to be human.

My accomplishments are a joke. I'm nothing. I'm nobody.

A part of me that tries to pull myself from the quicksand says, *The day is long; you can get out of this. Do your morning routine and then get out of the house and into the world. Don't camp out in these thoughts; pack up your tent and find a better view.*

I have my breakfast, take my shower, get dressed, try not to spend too much time in front of mirrors.

Soon I'm sitting in a coffee shop, attempting to float above the weight pulling on me, but it's not working. I get fixated on the negative thoughts. They won't shut up. Thoughts about how I'm such a loser and have no identity of my own—I only structure it around other people and their approval and my work, and that is pathetic. So pathetic. How can I be forty-five and still be stuck in this need for approval? I fixate on worry that I have no personality, that I have PTSD from childhood and will never feel good, never be more than a blank.

Tears and sniffles. I'm crying in a coffee shop, which adds yet another thing to my list of things I should feel bad about.

Then, another fixation:

That I should slap myself. I should slap myself in the face. I'm not speaking metaphorically or trying to be funny—I am fixated by the compulsion that I *must* slap myself in the face to release this feeling and then it will be better. Except I know it won't, because I've done it before, and it makes me feel so, so, so *sad*. It's *sad* that something in me responds to me feeling bad, feeling hurt, by wanting to hurt myself more.

The nice voice in my head says, *No, no. Please don't do that.*

So I sit for a while, work a little without any real focus.

The thought comes back, and finally I get up, go to the bathroom, and lock the door. I slap myself hard enough that I worry the people in the coffee shop can hear. I do it twice more. Wash my hands. Come back out.

Then I hate myself more for being so pathetic that I would do that.

Would I slap a child in the face? Because that's what I'm doing. I picture eight-year-old me, little Sara, as a person outside my body, and I'm just hauling off and slapping this child. Me.

It's too sad.

And also, it's embarrassing. It's so embarrassing to admit this here. I share a lot—and I mean a *lot*—about my life and feelings with my friends and husband. I've told my therapist nearly everything about me over the years. But this one thing, this one behavior, I can't confess. How do you say "I hit myself" and expect anyone to think of you the same again?

Weighted with the sadness and humiliation, I feel another compulsion:

What if I just screamed, right here in this coffee shop? Because that's what I want. I want to scream out my sadness

262

about what I just did to myself, just let a huge scream rip through me. What would happen? What would the people around me do?

I pack up and leave so I don't actually do it.

Walking home, I try to explore my fear, explore my feelings. I don't want to just shut myself down, because I know that one of my issues is that I can become so detached from myself and my feelings that it's like I'm not even inside my life. But also I don't want to feel *this*; I don't want to feel this way ever again. Even if it's just once in a while, it feels so terrible that it can become a shadow over every moment that I feel good.

My walk home takes me below a freeway overpass, and I consider letting that scream out, because no one would hear it. I don't do it, I think because I don't want to scare myself, and, honestly, I'm afraid I'll make my throat bleed if I scream as much as I want to. But when I get home, I scream into my pillow, cry until I throw up, slap myself again, and punch my leg so hard that I leave a bruise.

Nothing matters.

I'll always hate myself, and when I'm seventy-five I'll still be crying on a bed like this and will have wasted my life.

My books don't matter now. Having readers, having fans, having friends, none of it matters when I feel like this.

But what is "like this"? I don't know what I'm feeling; I don't know what I'm grieving or what I'm punishing myself for. It scares me when I'm like this, for a lot of reasons, one of which is: What message am I sending to my subconscious? That I deserve to be hurt? That I'm angry at myself about something. In the movies, on TV, people get slapped when they've crossed a line. People get slapped when the person slapping wants them to feel ashamed. People get slapped because words can't even express how frustrating and terrible they are.

I yell at nothing, maybe at God. I tell God that I've tried to be good, tried to do everything right, and I don't know what God wants from me. I don't know what *I* want from me.

The fact that I'm starting to defend myself is a good sign.

The next good sign is that I start thinking about how I will put this into words in my journal, how I would describe it in an essay like this. As soon as I get this narrative distance from the noise in my head, from the depressing story I'm telling myself about myself, I begin to come out of it.

I get up off the bed and go to my computer.

Thankfully, thankfully, these days are not common. Maybe once or twice a year, sometimes even more seldom. On a scale of one to ten, most days my anxieties sit somewhere between a two on a good day and an eight on a bad one. On terrible days like the one above, they're off the charts—ten times a thousand times infinity. I don't know exactly what's happening in my brain on those days to cause that magnification, but I do have some ideas of what's happening on any day they go over, say, a five or six.

It starts with the genetics. I was in a kind of group therapy once, and one thing we did was fill out our family tree
with all of the issues we knew about for every relative we
could think of. My father was a bipolar alcoholic, and at
least one of my grandfathers was an alcoholic, and there is
a lot of other depression and anxiety and addiction in my
family tree.

I highly recommend this exercise of doing your mental
health family tree because it takes a lot of the shame away.
I can look at the tree and say, "Oh, interesting. We're short,
stocky-limbed people with blue eyes, and we don't get cancer.
We have problems with food and weight, alcohol, parental
abandonment, and depression." I can look at the tree and
know that, actually, it would be surprising if I *didn't* have the
issues I have, given my gene pool. It's nothing personal, and
it's nothing I could have chosen to not have.

What I have learned is that the power I do have over the
genetics is self-care.

Do you know about self-care? It's what it sounds like:
taking care of yourself. Self-care is not just bubble baths and
me time. Self-care is about working (and it is work) to deeply
understand myself, my issues (inherited and otherwise), and
what I need to do in order to survive and thrive, and then
actually doing those things. Like, if you knew that half the
people in your family tree died young of a stroke, you'd do the
best you could to live in such a way to minimize your chances
of stroke. Or if all the men go bald by thirty, and you're a guy,

you'd work on accepting this and getting to like the shaved-head look.

Self-care isn't a cure. Self-care is an ongoing endeavor that sometimes you're good at and sometimes you're bad at, and it's trial and error, and a lot of times it's more gut than science, more intuition than prescription, more faith than facts. For me, self-care has been an empowering, exciting, frustrating, fascinating life project.

I'm tenacious and motivated by wanting to feel good or at least not terrible, and I will try almost anything. Over the last twenty years, that's included meditation, medication, special diets, talk therapy, one-on-one, group therapy, self-help books, alone time, people time, nature time, unplugged time, sleep management, exercise management, blood-sugar management, positive self-talk, journaling, massage, supplements, psychiatry. Maybe there's more stuff out there I haven't tried yet, and maybe someday I will. When my nice voice is talking, I know that I'm worth whatever it takes.

I've gotten to know myself well enough to put a basic self-care into place that almost always works. (If I do it—and sometimes I don't, either because circumstances don't allow it, or just because nobody is perfect.) The foundation of my self-care program is like a three-legged stool: diet, sleep, exercise. If those three things are in place, my stool is generally very steady.

There's a lot of anecdotal evidence and a fair amount of research on the impact of nutrition on mental health. A good diet for my brain is based on regular meals made up of whole foods, enough protein, not too many things made out of flour, *very* minimal sugar and junk food, and not too much caffeine or alcohol. One time I quit sugar and junk for six months straight, and I have never been less depressed or anxious. It was kind of amazing, actually. But it's hard to be perfect in that regard, and *another* important part of my self-care is not getting caught up in being perfect.

Sleep, for me, means like eight or preferably nine hours a night, and maybe a nap in the afternoon. I don't care if that seems like a lot! That's what helps me feel best. If I have a couple of nights in a row of much less than that, anxiety comes back strong. The amount isn't the same for everyone, but research backs up the fact that chronically not getting enough sleep messes with your brain chemistry, and . . . hello, anxiety.

Exercise does a lot of good for my mood, especially if it's exercise in nature, like a walk in a park or even in a pretty neighborhood, or near a beach or a mountain, if those happen to be handy. Science backs this one up too—in one study, ninety minutes of walking in nature actually decreased activity in the prefrontal cortex of the subjects' brains. That's the part of your brain and mine that's active during repetitive negative thoughts. There are also the endorphins that exercise releases, and the effects of deeper breathing and increased oxygen and daylight and all of that good stuff. I try to get out for at least one daily walk. It doesn't have to be sweaty or strenuous. (And in fact, if I'm doing it because I think I should be burning calories or something, it doesn't actually work that well to make me feel better.)

I learned all this by keeping a journal about what I ate, and how much sleep and exercise I got, and how I felt. That helped me make connections between my mind and my body and what worked best for me. When I find myself, for example, sitting in a coffee shop, fixated on hurting myself, or just generally having a day when the negative thoughts aren't that bad but are bad enough to ruin my day, I can almost always trace it back to something being off about my food, rest, or exercise. Maybe there were a bunch of days in a row when I binged on sugar or didn't leave the house or had crappy sleep or partied too much.

I feel very lucky that feeling good is this much in my control, that it works as well as the meds I've tried, because I know that's not true for everyone.

And there are still challenges.

One is, people just don't get it. Some things people have said to me: *You're not going to have some of the dessert I made you? It's just a piece of cake! Don't deprive yourself! Diet mentality is bad for you! Moderation, not deprivation!* I say I feel better without it; I say it's an antidepression diet; I say my stomach hurts; I say "no thank you" a hundred times; I say whatever it takes to get them off my back. Same goes for when people try to make me think I should function as well as they do on six hours of sleep, or they think I'm a drag for not partying.

Another thing is, life. Sometimes it isn't in your power to

eat the way you want or get the rest you need or get your alone time or time with people or whatever it is *you* need to feel better. Especially if you're living under someone else's roof and kind of living their lifestyle, even if you don't want to. If I know I'm going to be thrown into a circumstance where I'm not getting to make my preferred choices, I do the best I can and at least try to get my sleep. (The younger you are, the more this is probably the biggest challenge to self-care. If, for example, you're actually *living* with addicts or depressed or angry or anxious people who don't take care of themselves, it can be really tough. If you feel discouraged about it now, if everything around you works against what you know is good for you, know that it *gets so much better* when you get older and have more control over your environment. Meanwhile, do whatever you can to be good to yourself.)

Lastly, sometimes you just don't want to. Sometimes it sucks to feel high-maintenance, like if one little thing gets thrown off, you're going to fall apart. Sometimes you want to binge eat the sugar or party all night or spend a week on the couch. When that happens, and my mood symptoms show up, I do my best to remind myself that I won't feel this way forever. I'll try to talk to myself like I would to a friend: "You're tired. You need some good food and a good night's sleep, and you'll feel so much better after that." I try to treat myself very gently, and with respect. A lot of times this is enough to help me hold on until it comes true. Other times . . . well, I've told you what happens other times.

*   *   *

Your self-care plan will look different; it will be yours. Don't listen to anyone who says your method is dumb or won't work. Once you find something that works for you, respect it. And if it stops working, try something else. It's worth experimenting, learning, working at it, trying everything. We're worth feeling better by any means necessary.

Put On a Happy Face

by
Cynthia
Hand

When I was in high school, one of my friends used to talk about killing herself. She and I had been friends since we were toddlers; her grandparents lived right across the road from me, and she often came over to play when she was visiting them. By the time I was a teenager, I'd accumulated hundreds of memories of this girl: our little tan legs stretching under the sun on my backyard swing set, playing house and hide-and-seek and Barbies, laughing together at birthday parties, slurping ice pops on our back patio in the summertime. I'd known this girl for as long as I could remember. By high school we'd separated a little—we were a year apart in school and had different sets of friends and different interests and we lived in different parts of town—but I still considered her my friend. A good friend, even. Close.

That year, my senior year and her junior, she and I had an advanced French class together, which mostly entailed us being sent to the library to "translate" different French books into English. And, sometimes, as we sat dutifully writing out our terrible translations of *Le Petit Prince*, my friend talked about how she wanted to die. She spoke of her own death casually, the way a person might discuss vacation plans. She talked about how she would do it—by crashing her car or taking pills or cutting her wrists. It would be so simple, so easy, she said. If only she had the guts, she said, or wasn't so afraid of the pain, or didn't want to hurt people . . . she'd be gone.

I remember her talking about it. I can still call up the light tone she used, like it was no big deal, her killing herself. I vividly remember the way her eyes glittered strangely as she said the words. But what I don't remember, all these years later, is what *I* said to *her* when she talked about it, how I responded when she told me. I try to imagine it now—my eyes widening, tearing up as I tell her how much she meant to me, how awesome she was, how things were hard now but they'd get better—anything I could think to say to help her through the dark place she was in. I can picture hugging her. Walking her to the counselor's office. Getting help.

I can imagine it, but I don't remember it.

I don't remember doing anything when she told me. Most likely this is because I *didn't* do anything. I didn't tell anybody that my friend was in pain and needed help. I didn't try to help her myself.

Now, as an adult, I want to shake my teen self by the shoulders and scream, "What's wrong with you? Do something! DO SOMETHING!" *Why,* I wonder in amazement, *why didn't I do anything? Why didn't I listen?*

There are a few reasons, I think:

- I didn't take her seriously, not really. I thought she was just being dramatic. That's because I, too, occasionally thought about killing myself, but it was always in an abstract and completely theatrical way. I thought about it when I was hurting. My parents were going through a gnarly, painful divorce, and it seemed like they weren't even considering me or how I felt or what their choices were doing to me. I wanted them to know I was hurting, and then I'd think about how everyone would definitely know how much pain I was in if I killed myself. Suicide would be the ultimate statement, I thought. The problem with this was I didn't actually want to die. I just wanted people to notice my pain. So I assumed it was the same way for my friend (it wasn't) and she didn't want to kill herself so much as she wanted someone to pay attention to what was going on with her.

- My friend wasn't the sort of person who I thought of as being depressed. She actually seemed like a pretty happy person on the outside—she was always smiling, in fact. She had an infectious laugh that I could recognize from the other end of the school cafeteria. She told the most hilarious jokes. She was an A student. She didn't take drugs or drink too much at parties. She had friends. She had good parents, I thought. She didn't have any real reason to be unhappy, in my way of thinking. She didn't wear lots of eyeliner and dark lipstick and all-black clothes, which is how I assumed a "depressed teen" should look. She wasn't the type, I thought, who would actually kill herself.

- In spite of all my romantic/messed-up preconceptions, real-life, actual suicide was a foreign concept to me. It was what the bad guy did when he's finally caught and about to get arrested. It was a bathtub full of blood in a horror movie. It was a woman throwing herself under a train in classic literature. I didn't personally know anybody who'd committed suicide. Nobody ever talked about it, even though I grew up in Idaho, which has one of the highest suicide rates in the country. Suicide is the second leading cause of death for teens in Idaho, but in my mind, it was something that happened in other places, to other people. I couldn't imagine it happening in real life, to anyone I knew.

- I didn't want to get my friend in trouble. If I told someone about it, I knew there would be counselors and freaked-out parents and serious talks, and I didn't want my friend to have to go through the embarrassment of all of that over what was probably nothing, which brings us back to:

- I didn't really believe her.

So I was silent. I failed her.

My friend's still alive now, by the way, all grown-up with a cool job and a good life, and I am so glad—like cartwheels and the "Hallelujah Chorus" glad—she survived that time in high school. She lived. I talk to her now, and she says there are still hard times, but it's better. One of our other friends stepped up and told her parents about the way she was talking about dying. It was humiliating and horrible for a while, but she got help. And she made it through.

My younger brother didn't make it through. When he was seventeen (a junior in high school, while I was a junior in college), he killed himself with a hunting rifle.

Everyone who knew him was totally surprised and shocked. My brother was a popular guy at school. He was handsome—dark haired and athletic and strong. He was a member of the swim team and the ballroom dance team, and he'd dabbled with football and wrestling. He got good grades. He didn't drink or do drugs. He had loads of friends. He always seemed like he was in a good mood, always smiling, always cracking jokes.

My brother didn't look depressed. On the outside, he didn't appear to be fighting for his life. He seemed fine. Happy, even. He was very good at putting on a happy face.

I often wonder if my brother told his friends what he was thinking about, the way my friend told me in French class, but I doubt it. He kept things pretty close to the vest. He attempted suicide more than once before he died, and I talked to him about that, of course; I told him that I loved him, and I tried to understand why he would do such a thing, but neither one of us really knew what to say. It made us uncomfortable to talk about it. So we didn't. And then he was gone.

After he died, there were days when I'd have to duck into a bathroom to hide in a stall and quietly sob. I remember practicing the words "I'm good. How are you?" in the bathroom mirror so I could say those words convincingly when somebody asked me how I was. I switched to waterproof mascara. I didn't go out much. I hated meeting new people, because inevitably they would ask me where I was from and whether I had brothers and sisters. Then I'd have to choose whether to just say no, I was an only child, which was simpler but made me feel like I was betraying my brother, or to say that I had a brother and risk the follow-up questions that would reveal that he was dead.

"Oh my God, I'm so sorry," people would say when they found out, and then sometimes they'd ask, "How did he die?" and they always got the same expression when I told them—a mixture of pity and embarrassment and horror at themselves that they'd stumbled into such a morbid topic. And then there'd be an awkward silence while we tried to find a way to change the subject.

I hated that silence so much.

My grief wasn't exactly like the depression that my brother struggled with, but it came in similar, debilitating waves that left me unable to cope. I kept up my grades, but I didn't really care about my future anymore. I lost my sense of taste and smell for months. I experienced long periods of numbness in which I didn't feel anything at all, no happiness or sadness, which was almost worse than the moments when the loss of my brother felt like a real, tangible hole being ripped out of my chest. There were panic attacks. There were days I was so worn out from the grief that it seemed like a huge effort to open my eyes and get out of bed. I wanted to sleep all day, because when I was asleep, I could exist in a place where my brother was still alive. Then there were nights I couldn't sleep, and I'd think of how much simpler it would be if I could just stop everything. If only I had the guts, or wasn't so afraid of the pain, or didn't want to hurt the people in my life who were already hurting so much.

For about two years after his death, I was really, really not okay.

In some ways, seventeen years later, I am still not okay. I don't know if I ever will be. Time does help—slowly, slowly it helps—but I will never be the same as I was before. And back then, after it happened, I didn't talk about it. One thing

I learned very early on was that my pain made other people uncomfortable, so I tried to hide it. Inside, I was a tiny boat in the middle of an ocean under a big, black storm, but on the outside, I seemed like just a normal college student, eating lunch in the cafeteria and going to class and making jokes.

I put on a happy face.

I wish I had some incredible insight about how to get through pain. I don't. I don't feel like I've gained much in the way of wisdom through it all. There's no happy cure, no easy way to navigate through the hard stuff but to keep rowing the stupid little boat. But I will say this: The happy face might make other people more comfortable around you, but something that will really help *you* is to get to that moment when your friend says, "How are you?" and you tell them the truth—that you're not okay.

People can't help you if they don't know. Don't put on a happy face. Show them your real face.

And if someone tells you that they're hurting, listen to them. Take them seriously. You just might be handing someone a flashlight that will help them make it through the dark, dark night.

My Two-Headed Monster Friend

by Francisco X. Stork

When I was fourteen years old, I lived for two months with three saints. Charlie Stork, my adoptive father, had died the year before in an automobile accident, and my mother was back in Mexico taking care of her ailing father. Father Martinez, our parish priest, volunteered to take me in. There was a storage room in the rectory that could be converted into a bedroom by placing an army cot and clearing off an old desk. The desk chair would also serve as a nightstand, and the desk lamp could be moved to the chair for night reading. Surrounding the army cot stood life-size statues of Ignatius Loyola, Francis Xavier, and Martín de Porres. With the lights out it was hard to remember that they were not real.

The four priests who lived in the rectory led quiet lives. They spent the days in various churches around El Paso and came home for a light supper, an hour or so of TV, and then off to their rooms. By eight p.m. the house, which resembled a wing of a small hotel, was eerily quiet. I did my homework. I read. I played a form of basketball in my room with a tennis ball and a coffee can. I envied the priests for the easy friendship they had with solitude.

Despite the presence of my three mute friends, or maybe because of their presence, I was never scared. Or maybe I should say that I didn't have the kind of fear that people have of ghosts or other supernatural beings. What I did fear was that the loneliness I felt would never go away.

Sometimes loneliness comes when you miss someone. I felt that kind of loneliness for my adoptive father. I first met Charlie Stork when I was six years old. A retired American citizen born in the Netherlands, he was traveling through Mexico when he met Ruth Arguelles, a single mother. Charlie married my mother, adopted me, and gave me his last name. Soon after that, he brought his new family to El Paso, Texas. In the seven years that I knew him, Charlie went from the stranger who was taking me away from my grandfather's house to the father I always wanted to have. I was just beginning to feel certain that he would never abandon me when one evening a policeman came to tell me that Charlie had died instantaneously in an automobile accident.

But besides the loneliness of missing someone you love or hope to love, loneliness can also be a kind of bereft desolation—the feeling of being the only one left in a universe that doesn't know you're there. And joined to this painful sense of aloneness is a desperate longing for someone's, anyone's love. It is this second kind of loneliness that I felt for the first time there, surrounded by my stony friends.

I mention loneliness now as I write about the depression and mania involved in the illness we call bipolar disorder because after many years of reflection, I believe that those two months in that sometimes suffocating solitude were when the seeds of the illness first appeared. It took me a long time to discover that the sadness and isolation I felt then was a malfunction of my brain: depression. But it took even longer to recognize that along with the sadness and isolation there was an intense and restless energy, an insatiable wanting for some kind of love that would fill the void carved out by emptiness. Emptiness and longing are the twin, inseparable brothers of bipolar disorder.

My three saints seemed kind enough, but they could not give me what I needed. Nor could Father Martinez or the other priests comfort my emptiness, even if I had somehow found the courage to tell them what I was feeling. When my mother returned from Mexico, the emptiness and longing persisted. It continued through high school and college, until one day in graduate school the pull of these two forces became so powerful and so unbearable that the only thing I could do to stop them was to end my life.

The term "depression" acquired a new significance in the days that followed the impulsive but strangely calculated act that seemed to have been performed by someone I did not know. While I lay at Harvard's Stillman Infirmary, wondering where I would be if my roommate's sister hadn't unexpectedly returned and found me unable to wake up, I began to see the connection between the suicide attempt and the hopelessness that preceded it. But, for some reason, I failed to take the desperate wishing and craving that also accompanied it as something related to, but different from, the hopelessness. It was almost as if lack of hope and unreasonable hope for something nameless and unattainable were so bound up together I could not pull them apart. Whatever this craving-like hope sought, the only thing certain about it was that it could not be found or possessed in this here life. It was not until some thirty-five years later that it came to me that I was dealing with a two-headed monster, and it is only now, as a sixty-three-year-old man, that I am finding out that the monster can be tamed, not completely, but enough to let me live.

During those thirty-five years, I stumbled along, somehow managing to earn a living in a variety of legal jobs and even, miraculously it now seems, finding a way to write creatively. I did what I could to treat the depression I thought afflicted me with the help of therapists and antidepressants and alcohol. I went from one job to another, sometimes leaving them out of boredom, and at other times being asked to leave. If I did not lose my family during this time, it was only because my wife and son and daughter saw glimpses of goodness in me that I did not.

When I was fifty-five years old, I walked into the Bipolar Clinic of Massachusetts General Hospital. I'm not exactly

sure what rock-bottom behavior led me to the door of someone who could help me understand not so much the sadness
but the impulsivity behind actions that were causing so much
pain to myself, yes, but mostly to others. Maybe it was my
dear wife's "I can't do this anymore." Or maybe it was the car
I crashed into a tree. Or maybe it was my coworker who found
me drunk on the floor of my office and who firmly told me that
I was on the verge of losing another job.

The process of determining whether I had bipolar disorder gradually made me more aware of what was truly
happening inside me when I did things that seemed so "out
of character" for the person everyone thought I was. For
example, I had always seen my secret drinking as an exten-
sion of depression—something I did to bring me back to life,
as it were. Like other depressed persons, I hung on to the
term "self-medication" to lessen my own responsibility with
alcohol. But when I looked carefully, when I really examined
how I felt as I waited for the lunch hour to come around so
I could find a dark, cool bar, I didn't see a depressed person
struggling out of his desk chair and ambling to a bar to drown
his sorrows. I saw a man who couldn't sit still possessed by a
painful restlessness that sought the quietude of alcohol. And
little by little, I saw the rest of the manic behavior—all the
harmful, hurtful acts I did out of that hunger born of loneliness first experienced when I was fourteen years old.

I am fortunate to have slowly and with help found the
right medication and just the right dosage. I am fortunate also

to have gained a level of awareness good enough to recognize loneliness and longing, the two-headed monster that lives within me. Sometimes, just when I think I have befriended the monster, he reminds me of his power. Then I have to let him know that I know he exists, that he is part of me, that he will be with me forever. Like a child, he wants attention. But like a father, I let him know that I'm in charge.

When I talk about bipolar disorder, I use words like "loneliness" and "uncontrollable longing" rather than words like "depression" and "mania" because the former are more descriptive of what I actually feel, even though depression is a bundle of feelings and thoughts more complicated than loneliness, and mania is more than irrepressible longing. "Loneliness" and "longing" also remind me that despite its danger, the illness is more than a medical condition. It is part of me, for better or for worse. Giving it a human face, calling it the things I felt when I was fourteen years old, helps me to look at my limited and flawed humanity with kindness.

I am not a person who believes I am depressed because I am somehow special. I'm not more sensitive or more artistic than those who are not mentally ill. Nor do I believe in the powers of productivity and creativity that are sometimes attributed to mania. Or rather, I don't believe that what I do under those conditions is my best work or even the kind of work I want to do. Now and then I meet people with bipolar disorder who tell me that they stopped taking their medication because it was dulling their creativity. All I can do is think that they have not been truly depressed or truly manic. Depression and mania exist on a continuum above which it is possible to function with painful consequences (like I did for many years) and below which it is simply not possible to do anything that requires thought or imagination or logic. A manic state is chaotic, and what seems like the fire of inspiration is a delusional and egocentric babble, a mixture of arrogance and ignorance that confuses gibberish with art.

And yet, despite all this, I think that loneliness and longing point to an aspect of our soul that needs our care and our attention. We live in a society where each of us can feel more and more not just alone but lonely despite our myriad technological connections and our virtual "friends." The loneliness we feel points to that part of our soul that needs to have genuine and true friends, the kind of friendship that is soul to soul, generous, and does not seek anything other than the joy and support of friendship. And the longing? Ah, the longing. I think the wild craving is a reminder that what our society sometimes offers us is not enough. Deep down we want something truer and more valuable than what so many of us spend our lives wanting and seeking and sometimes finding, only to discover more emptiness. The longing is for meaning and purpose in our lives, to do something only we can do. Our wanting explodes into hellish and manic activity when we feed it with the trivial and the banal. Our heart's yearning will find its peace and its hoped-for enthusiasm when it humbly seeks and finds something greater than ourselves.

It All Ends Here

by Jessica Burkhart

This is the umpteenth time I've tried to write this piece. I thought it would be done in one fell swoop—share my story of anxiety and *boom*! Done. But no. This is a million times harder than anything I've ever written. Writing this piece is more demanding than writing a fifty-thousand-word manuscript in three weeks—which I've done several times. Even now, I'm dancing around the actual story with this preface. Okay, it's time to stop hiding and just write already.

I was always an anxious kid. In elementary school and middle school, I threw up almost every morning before class. Every. Day. I homeschooled for high school, so the vomiting stopped, but I had to constantly be doing something I deemed "productive." My father lost his job when I was thirteen, and I felt an overwhelming sense of "I have to help my family survive." The only thing I'd ever been good at was writing, so I sent terrible query letters to dozens of magazines and got rejection after rejection. Finally, at fourteen, I got my first check: five dollars and it paid for McDonald's—a luxury for us. I was hooked. After that, even if it was midnight and I was watching a late-night show, I had to be working on a magazine article or studying.

At twenty-two I moved to Brooklyn, New York. It was 2009, and I hit the height of my anxiety. I couldn't leave my apartment. Or order food, unless I did it online, and even then I didn't want to talk to the delivery guys. All I wanted to do was work on my book series—Canterwood Crest—something that was going to pay my rent and keep me from ending up on the street. So I worked. Hard. All the time.

My then best friend noticed that I couldn't stop working and offered me a Xanax. She said she took them to quiet her brain. That sounded like pure bliss, but I doubted it would work for me. I took the pill anyway, and for the next half hour I watched a rerun of *The Hills* with my bestie. Not once did I pull out a notebook and jot down ideas for my book. Not once did I turn on my phone and add to my to-do list. I simply enjoyed the drama between Lauren Conrad and her friends! (Can I just say how thankful I am that DVDs of *The Hills* exist for today's viewing pleasure?!)

I went to see a psychiatrist—the same one my friend saw—and he immediately prescribed me a half milligram of Xanax once or twice a day as needed. I usually took the pill in the evening, when business hours were over and I wanted to go out with my friends. Xanax allowed me to do that. I could go bar hopping and not worry about work. I could talk to strangers. Flirt with the bartenders. Xanax made me feel "normal."

I was able to make all my book deadlines, but still wind down at night. Over the next few months, the timing of when I took my daily Xanax changed. I started waking up out of breath and feeling like I was having a heart attack. My chest constricted so painfully that I couldn't think straight. So I took a Xanax at seven thirty in the morning. My symptoms went away after about ten minutes, and I went on with my day. I took a second Xanax that evening and felt back on track. This happened the next morning and, again, I took a Xanax.

Before I even got out of bed over the next few months, I'd dry swallow my Xanax from the pill case that now resided beside my pillow. Once my panic passed, I got up and faced the day. But the morning pill wasn't erasing all of my panic like it used to. I saw my psychiatrist, and he said that I was building a tolerance to the drug and that was normal. So he upped my dose to one and a half milligrams a day. No big deal.

Within a few months I was up to two milligrams a day.

Then two and a quarter.

Two and a half.

Time was still passing, and I needed more. I couldn't breathe without it.

Two and three-quarters.

Then three.

But it's still not totally helping my panic, I told my psychiatrist.

Three and a quarter.

Three and a half.

Three and three-quarters.

My doctor didn't tell me that the "average" Xanax user takes a half milligram daily or as needed. I was now dependent on the drug, and my tolerance grew with every month or so that passed.

Now I was at four.

Four and a quarter.

Four and a half.

Four and three-quarters.

Pause. Holy shit. Now I took it first thing in the morning, at lunch, and at night. My life revolved around when I could take my next dose. My *heart* knew the time because it began thundering in my chest, and I started sweating by one in the afternoon if I haven't taken my afternoon pill. It felt like a white-hot fireplace poker seared a hole into my chest unless I took my pill. I felt like I was going to die if I didn't take it.

And no, not again. The pill wasn't as effective as it was last month. What the fuck. I needed to take more. That's what it was for, right?

So I took five milligrams that day. My psychiatrist upped it.

Five and a quarter.

Five and a half.

Five and three-quarters.

By 2010 I was on six milligrams of Xanax a day. S-I-X. Some days I took eight, nine, or ten milligrams if I was having a particularly bad day. Something else my psych didn't tell me? Xanax messes with your short-term memory if you take large doses. My memory was shot. I had to write down everything. It became hard to write a series because I couldn't keep facts in my brain. I'd repeat information to friends and didn't even realize I was doing so.

I didn't even know that I was on a crazy high dosage. It's from a doctor, so there couldn't be anything wrong with that, right? Wrong. But that part comes later.

It was a gross gray day in February of 2010 when I called to schedule an appointment to see my doctor. I needed a Xanax refill.

"I'm sorry, but Dr. X is on vacation for the rest of the week," the overly cheery receptionist informed me. "I'll put you down for Monday, though."

I hung up, panic filling my body. It was Tuesday. It felt as though someone had punched me in the stomach. I would be out of pills tomorrow. What was I supposed to do?

I called my friend, and she gave me the leftover pills she had, but they were half milligrams, and I chewed through them like candy. She advised me to get online and see what people did when they ran out of Xanax. While I did that, Bestie went through our Rolodex of friends to see if any had spare pills or knew where I could buy some. It turned out that there were plenty of other pills for sale, but none that I needed. Online,

I found a forum, well, multiple forums of people who used Xanax. I posted a question:

Hi, I'm on six mgs of Xanax a day and I'm out tmrw. I can't see my doctor until Monday. Will I go through withdrawal? What should I do?

The replies were fast. And terrifying.

Most people told me to stretch the pills until my next appointment. They all said I'd have severe withdrawal—chills, aches, vomiting, headaches, sweating—and more if I didn't get even a tiny bit of Xanax in my body every day. They told me to take an antihistamine to help with symptoms, but to be prepared. Xanax messes with you, they said; it plays hardball.

The scariest comments came from those who had gone through Xanax withdrawal. These posters said I could have a seizure if I wasn't careful, and I should really consider going to the ER. Those same posters also said I'd be looked at as an addict and wouldn't be given anything more than a saline drip and maybe antinausea meds if I was lucky.

The ER was out. I couldn't stomach the thought of someone calling me an addict.

I counted my pills and wrote the total in my planner. Like the writer I am, I wanted to keep track of what I was going to take and note my symptoms every day. I had five pills to last me from Wednesday to Monday. Six days. Normally, I would have taken eighteen pills in that time span.

Wednesday morning, I took one milligram and felt slightly uncomfortable all day. My discomfort grew as the day progressed. I had my evening cocktail—a cosmo—around two in the afternoon because I needed something to dull my chest pains. I waited as long as I could, until eight or nine in the evening, before taking one more milligram. I barely slept that night.

Thursday morning I took a milligram. I was nauseous and didn't eat anything all day. I couldn't focus on work. All I could think about was the pain in my chest. I kept checking my pulse and felt my heart beat faster with every hour that passed. My palms and the bottoms of my feet sweated. Everything either pissed me off or made me cry.

I spent the wee hours of Friday morning with my head in the toilet. Dry heaving for hours. I hadn't eaten since Wednesday, and there was nothing to throw up. I forced vanilla vodka—which I haven't had since—down my throat in an effort to try to sleep. I took double and triple amounts of over-the-counter sleeping pills. I added prescription sleeping pills from another friend. Nothing worked, though. I wanted to sleep until Monday.

By the time Saturday dragged on, I was an immobile lump on my bed. I half watched TV with the volume off because anything above a whisper was too loud. Sometimes the TV's motion made me feel sick. I lay on top of my pink comforter and saw something move out of the corner of my eye. I had *zero* energy to get up, but if THAT was what I thought it was, I needed a can of Raid ASAP. I started to get up, and suddenly the bug—the *cockroach*—I'd seen on the corner of the wall moved to the wall in front of me. Now there wasn't just one. They were multiplying. Cockroaches covered my wall. How the fuck had I let things get this bad? I'd never, ever had a roach in my apartment, and now it was swarming with the vile insects. I struggled off the bed, standing on shaky legs, and half crawled to the kitchen for a can of bug spray. I wanted to scream, but I had no voice. I doubted if I had to call 911 that I'd even be able to get out my name. I was just so tired, and none of my body was working the way it was supposed to.

I glanced back at the wall. The bugs were gone. I blinked and rubbed my eyes. Every last bug was gone. I stayed on the kitchen floor for God knows how long until I had the energy to crawl back to bed. That was the first of several hallucinations.

I spent that day wishing I would die. I wasn't suicidal—I simply wanted my heart to stop so what felt like this agonizingly slow death would end. I felt trapped in my body. I couldn't move or speak. Even my hair hurt. My teeth felt as though they were being pulled out with pliers. My skin didn't like the touch of anything. If I brushed my arm against a pillow, it felt like a thousand tiny electric shocks to my body.

I didn't write down anything on Sunday. I just know my best friend came over and spent the night with me because she was worried.

Monday morning I managed to get from my apartment to a waiting car and take a half-hour drive to midtown Manhattan to my doctor's office. I remember very little about that appointment except that he looked scared. He apologized over and over before helping me out the door with my prescription in hand. I walked, though I don't know how, to the mom-and-pop pharmacy that knew me and took five minutes to fill my prescription. I bought a Snapple from the pharmacy and popped ten milligrams of Xanax at the counter.

Within minutes my headache ceased. My body stopped shaking. My stomach settled. My vision cleared. My heartbeat slowed. I stood there, swiped my debit card, and left. I felt as though I'd spent days on a treadmill without one break. I had severe lingering chest pain like my heart had bruised the inside of my body from beating so hard. On the train ride back to Brooklyn, I felt sore but elated. I was finally okay. It was over. I'd never cut a doctor appointment so close again.

So I resumed taking six milligrams of Xanax every day. Flash forward to now. I have a new psychiatrist, who, when I told him what I'd gone through, asked me how I was still alive. He said I shouldn't be. I made the decision to start coming off Xanax. I'm missing too much, and my body keeps wanting more. As I write this, I'm in the first stage of cutting back. I'm on five and three-quarters milligrams a day. I'll take that dosage for a week then try five and a half milligrams for a week and so on. One doctor thought I could come off Xanax in three weeks. Wrong. I could, but not safely. The doctor I chose, the doctor I trust, has me on a six-to-eight-month cutback schedule. My motto is just like that of Alcoholics Anonymous: one day at a time.

The teensy cutback has made me uncomfortable. My

chest aches. My heart's beating a little faster than normal, and sometimes it's hard to ignore. I'm on day seven of my plan. Will I make it to day eight? I hope so. I want to be off Xanax, or at the very least down to a much lower dosage. But a relapse isn't out of the question. I fight with myself every few hours when my chest burns, and I know if I *just* took that quarter of a pill it would make me feel okay.

I get angry. I have a doctor who is willing to give me six milligrams a day. Why not just take it and live my life? Deep down, I know the answer. Because I'm not really living. My life revolves around a flower-covered bag of pills that I have to tote everywhere. My body is a slave to the clock. I'm tired of it.

I can't go back to six. I won't. I'm not going back to a place where, if my doctor happens to be away, I start to see cockroaches on my walls. Never again. My Xanax dependence and addiction ends here. One day at a time.

Resources

If you have questions or want more information, here are some websites to help you find answers:

NAMI (National Alliance on Mental Illness)
www.nami.org

Mental Health America
www.mentalhealthamerica.net

National Suicide Prevention Lifeline
www.suicidepreventionlifeline.org
and 800-273-TALK (8255)

US Department of Health and Human Services
www.mentalhealth.gov

Acknowledgments

Thank you to Zac Brewer for encouraging this idea from day one.

Lots of gratitude to Shaun David Hutchinson, Melissa Marr, and several other lovely people who shared their experiences with anthologies. I'm so grateful for all your help especially in those early days.

Thanks to Ed Maxwell for helping me through this process.

Much gratitude to Josh Getzler. You've been nothing short of incredibly supportive while I've worked on this book.

Bethany Buck, I can't thank you enough for taking on this project. Your endless enthusiasm, support, and friendship means so much. Publishing wouldn't be publishing without you.

I couldn't be happier that Pulse picked up this collection. Simon & Schuster is my home, and there's no place I'd rather have backing this book. Thank you to Elizabeth Mims and Brian Luster for the detailed copyedits. Many thanks to sales and marketing folks for your support. Also, many thanks to Steve Scott and the art department for the brilliant cover!

Fiona Simpson, you're always a joy to work with and I so appreciate you letting me take the reins while still offering guidance. Being an editor is much more difficult than I'd imagined, but it's also so wonderful. You made this first experience as perfect as could be, and I hope to find myself in the editor role again.

Thank you to all my friends and family who have given me strength during my own journey.

Finally, thank you to the talented authors who shared your stories with me. Writing this essay probably wasn't the *most* fun writing project you've ever had, but each of you understood how your words and your voices would impact the lives of so many.

About the Authors

E. KRISTIN ANDERSON is a poet and author living in Austin, TX. She is the coeditor of *Dear Teen Me,* an anthology based on the popular website, and editor of *Hysteria: Writing the Female Body,* from Lucky Bastard Press. Kristin is the author of eight chapbooks of poetry including *A Guide for the Practical Abductee* (Red Bird Chapbooks); *Pray, Pray, Pray: Poems I wrote to Prince in the middle of the night* (Porkbelly Press); *Fire in the Sky* (Grey Book Press); *She Witnesses* (dancing girl press & studio); and *We're Doing Witchcraft* (Hermeneutic Chaos Press). Kristin recently took a position as Special Projects Manager for ELJ and is a poetry editor at *Found Poetry Review.* Once upon a time she worked at the *New Yorker.* Find her online at EKristinAnderson.com and on twitter at @ek_anderson.

JENNIFER L. ARMENTROUT, a #1 *New York Times* and #1 international bestselling author of young adult, new adult, and adult fiction, doesn't quite know how to take time off from writing. So she spends her days writing contemporary, paranormal, thrillers and suspense, and fantasy. Of course, all of her stories have more than a touch of romance to them.

CYN BALOG is the author of *Unnatural Deeds* (Sourcebooks, 2016), and six other YA novels. She lives in Pennsylvania with her husband and daughters. Visit her online at CynBalog.com.

AMBER BENSON is a writer, director, actor, and maker of things. She wrote the Calliope Reaper-Jones urban fantasy series for Ace/Roc and the middle-grade book *Among the Ghosts* for Simon & Schuster. She codirected the Slamdance feature *Drones,* and (cowrote) and directed the BBC animated series *The Ghosts of Albion.* She also spent three years as Tara Maclay on the television series *Buffy the Vampire Slayer.* Her latest book is *The End of Magic.*

FRANCESCA LIA BLOCK is the author of more than twenty-five books of fiction, nonfiction, short stories, and poetry. FrancescaLiaBlock.com.

JESSICA BURKHART wrote her first novel at nineteen years old. That book, *Take the Reins,* spawned a twenty-book series, Canterwood Crest, which to date has over one million copies in print and is published in Portuguese, French, and Polish. Jess also wrote the chapter book series Unicorn Magic (Simon & Schuster) and a young adult novel *Wild Hearts* (Bloomsbury). For more, visit Jess online at JessicaBurkhart.com or tweet her @JessicaBurkhart.

CRISSA-JEAN CHAPPELL was born in Miami, Florida, and now lives in Brooklyn, New York. Her debut YA novel, *Total Constant Order* (HarperTeen), is an NYPL Book for the Teen Age and a *VOYA* Perfect Ten. Chappell's second novel, *Narc* (Flux Books), is currently optioned for film. *More Than Good*

Enough (Flux Books) is a Florida Book Awards medalist, which *Kirkus* calls "compelling and emotionally nuanced." *Snowbirds* (Merit Press, 2016) is her most recent novel. Chappell is a professor of creative writing and cinema studies. When she misses South Florida, she talks to the wild parrots in Prospect Park.

SARAH FINE is the author of several books for teens, including *Of Metal and Wishes* (McElderry/Simon & Schuster) and its sequel, *Of Dreams and Rust*; the Guards of the Shadowlands YA urban fantasy series (Skyscape/Amazon Children's Publishing); and *The Impostor Queen* (McElderry, January 2016). She's also the coauthor (with Walter Jury) of two YA sci-fi thrillers published by Putnam/Penguin: *Scan* and its sequel, *Burn*. Her first adult urban fantasy romance series, Servants of Fate, includes *Marked*, *Claimed*, and *Fated*, all published by 47North in 2015, and her second adult UF series—*The Reliquary*—kicks off in summer 2016.

KELLY FIORE-STULTZ has a BA in English from Salisbury University and an MFA in poetry from West Virginia University. Her first young adult novel, *Taste Test*, was released in August 2013 from Bloomsbury USA, and her second, *Just Like the Movies*, again from Bloomsbury, was released in 2014. *Thicker Than Water* was published by HarperTeen in 2016. Kelly lives and teaches in West Virginia with three children, two dogs, one hedgehog, and a very patient and loving husband. You can connect with Kelly at her website: kellyfiorewrites.com and on Twitter: @KFioreStultz.

CANDACE GANGER is a young adult author, ghostwriter for award-winning nonfiction and bestselling fiction authors, and contributing writer for Hello Giggles (a site cofounded by actress Zooey Deschanel, with over one million Facebook followers), garnering interest from *The Steve Harvey Show*. She worked previously as assistant editor for phys.org and is an avid supporter of TWLOHA and The Bully Project. Her current novel, *The Inevitable Collision of Birdie & Bash*, will be out via St. Martin's Press (Summer 2017).

MEGAN KELLEY HALL, writer, literary publicist, and antibullying advocate based north of Boston, is the author of *Sisters of Misery* and *The Lost Sister*. She has written for a variety of national publications, including *Elle*, *Glamour*, *Boston Magazine*, *Parenting*, *American Baby*, *Huffington Post*, and *Working Mother*. Hall is coeditor (along with *New York Times* bestselling author Carrie Jones) of the critically acclaimed anthology about bullying entitled *Dear Bully: 70 Authors Tell Their Stories*. She is currently hard at work on her next teen thriller. MeganKelleyHall.com.

CYNTHIA HAND is the *New York Times* bestselling author of several books for teens, including the Unearthly trilogy, the contemporary novel *The Last Time We Say Goodbye*, and a coauthor of the new historical comedy *My Lady Jane*. Before turning to writing for young adults, she studied literary fiction and earned both an MFA and a PhD in fiction writing.

She and her family divide their time between Idaho and California, where she teaches creative writing and literature at Pepperdine University.

ELLEN HOPKINS is the NYT bestselling author of *Crank, Burned, Impulse, Glass, Identical, Tricks, Fallout, Perfect, Triangles, Tilt,* and *Collateral.* She lives in Carson City, Nevada, with her husband and grandson. She can be visited at EllenHopkins.com.

MAUREEN JOHNSON is the *New York Times* bestselling author of over a dozen YA novels, including *Suite Scarlett, The Name of the Star,* and *13 Little Blue Envelopes.* She can be found at MaureenJohnsonBooks.com and on Twitter @maureenjohnson.

TARA KELLY adores variety in her life. In addition to being an author, she's a one-girl band, graphic designer, videographer, photographer, and avocado addict. You can usually find her hiking in the Rockies or chasing thunderstorms. She lives in Colorado with her sound design master husband and two gigantic, fluffy cats. Find out more about her books at: TheTaraTracks.com.

KAREN MAHONEY is the author of *The Iron Witch, The Wood Queen,* and *The Stone Demon,* which make up a YA contemporary fantasy trilogy for Flux in the US and Random

House in the UK. *Falling to Ash* (September 2012) began a new series for Random House UK about an ass-kicking teen vampire called Moth. You can read more of Moth's adventures in her very own webcomic: KazMahoney.com.

MELISSA MARR, a former literature teacher who lives in Arizona, is the author of young adult fantasy novels. Her first, the *New York Times* bestseller *Wicked Lovely*, was published in 2007. It was followed by *Ink Exchange, Fragile Eternity, Radiant Shadows, Darkest Mercy*, "Stopping Time" and "Old Habits." Her *Faery Tales & Nightmares* is a collection of stories for young people. A manga series also is set in Marr's Wicked Lovely fantasy world. Marr's first book for adult readers was *Graveminder*, which *Publishers Weekly* called "a quirky dark fantasy fashioned around themes of fate, free will—and zombies." Marr also coedited her first anthology, *Enthralled*, published the e-book *Lovestruck*, and published her non-series young adult novel, *Untamed City: Carnival of Secrets*.

KIMBERLY McCREIGHT is the author of the *New York Times* bestseller *Reconstructing Amelia*, which was nominated for the Edgar, Anthony, and Alex awards; and the *USA Today* bestseller *Where They Found Her*. The first book in her YA trilogy, The Outliers, is forthcoming in May. She attended Vassar College and graduated cum laude from the University of Pennsylvania Law School. She lives in Brooklyn with her husband and two daughters.

HANNAH MOSKOWITZ is a tank top–collecting, TV-obsessed, *Rocky Horror*–performing woman of mystery. She's a '90s kid, a mezzo-soprano, and a professional Sims-breeder. She's the author of several books for young adults, including *Break*; *Invincible Summer*; *Zombie Tag*; *Gone, Gone, Gone* (a Stonewall Honor book); *Teeth*; *Marco Impossible*; and *Not Otherwise Specified*.

SCOTT NEUMYER is a journalist who has been published by the *New York Times*, *Rolling Stone*, *Wall Street Journal*, *Sports Illustrated*, *ESPN*, *GQ*, *Esquire*, *Wired*, *Men's Fitness*, and many more publications. His 2013 story "I Am Royce White: Living and Working with Anxiety Disorder" won the American Society of Journalists and Authors' Award in the First-Person Narrative category. He is currently an editor for 22Words.com and continues to freelance for many publications. He lives in central New Jersey with his wife, two daughters, and two cats. @ScottNeumyer.

LAUREN OLIVER is the cofounder of content development company Paper Lantern Lit. She is also the *New York Times* bestselling author of various novels for teens, including *Delirium*, *Before I Fall*, *Panic*, and *Vanishing Girls*. A graduate of the University of Chicago and NYU's MFA program, Lauren Oliver divides her time between New York, Connecticut, and a variety of airport lounges. You can visit her online at LaurenOliverBooks.com.

APRILYNNE PIKE is a critically acclaimed #1 *New York Times* bestselling author who has been spinning tales since she was a child with a hyperactive imagination. At the age of twenty she received her BA in Creative Writing from Lewis-Clark State College in Lewiston, Idaho. When not writing, Aprilynne can usually be found out running; she also enjoys singing, acting, reading, and working with pregnant moms as a childbirth educator doula. Aprilynne lives in Arizona with her husband and four kids; she is enjoying the sunshine.

TOM POLLOCK is a graduate of the Sussex University Creative Writing Programme, and a member of the London-based writers' group The T Party. He has lived everywhere from Scotland to Sumatra, but the peculiar magic of London has always drawn him back. You can find Tom online at TomPollock.com and @tomhpollock.

AMY REED is the author of the edgy contemporary YA novels *Beautiful, Clean, Crazy, Over You, Damaged, Invincible,* and *Unforgivable.* Her new book *The Nowhere Girls,* about three misfit girls who start an underground movement to avenge the rape of a classmate and overthrow the misogynist culture at their school, was published in fall 2017 by Simon Pulse. She lives in Asheville, North Carolina. You can find her online at AmyReedFiction.com.

CINDY L. RODRIGUEZ was a newspaper reporter for the *Hartford Courant* and a researcher for the *Boston Globe* before becoming a public school teacher. She is now a reading specialist at a Connecticut middle school and an adjunct professor at a community college. She is also a founding member of Latinxs in Kid Lit and was a team member of We Need Diverse Books. She lives in Connecticut with her young daughter and rescued mutt. Her debut novel is *When Reason Breaks* (Bloomsbury 2015).

FRANCISCO X. STORK was born in Mexico. He moved to El Paso, Texas, with his adoptive father and mother when he was nine. He attended Spring Hill College, Harvard University, and Columbia Law School. He worked as an attorney for thirty-three years before retiring in 2015. He is married and has two grown children and one beautiful granddaughter. His most recent novel, *The Memory of Light* (Scholastic), received starred reviews from *Kirkus*, *Publishers Weekly*, *Booklist*, and *School Library Journal*. FranciscoStork.com.

WENDY TOLIVER is the best-selling, award-winning author of five novels for young adults, including two based on the ABC TV hit drama *Once Upon a Time: Red's Untold Tale* and *Regina Rising*. She lives with her husband, three sons, two dogs, two cats, and a bearded dragon in a Utah town so small there isn't even a traffic light. Surrounded by ski resorts, a lake, a river, and trails, there's always something exciting to do outdoors. But she also enjoys staying inside, where she likes reading, writing, and baking. To find out more, visit her website: WendyToliver.com.

DAN WELLS writes in a variety of genres, from dark humor to science fiction to supernatural thriller. Born in Utah, he spent his early years reading and writing. He is the author of the Partials series and the John Cleaver series. He has been nominated for both the Hugo and the Campbell Award, and has won two Parsec Awards for his podcast, *Writing Excuses*. TheDanWells.com.

ROBISON WELLS is the author of *Blackout*, *Dead Zone*, *Variant*, *Feedback*, *Dark Energy*, and *Airships of Camelot*. *Variant* was a *Publishers Weekly* Best Book, a YALSA Quick Pick for Reluctant Readers, and an international bestseller. Robison lives in the Rocky Mountains, with mountain goats out the front windows and elk pastures just down the road.

RACHEL M. WILSON grew up in Birmingham, Alabama. She studied theater at Northwestern and earned her MFA in writing for children and young adults from Vermont College of Fine Arts. Wilson's debut novel *Don't Touch* (HarperTeen) received praise for its treatment of obsessive-compulsive disorder. Her devoted pup, Remy Frankenstein, helps her remember to sleep. RachelMWilsonbooks.com.

SARA ZARR is the acclaimed author of six novels for young adults, including *How to Save a Life* and *Story of a Girl*. She's a National Book Award finalist and two-time Utah Book Award winner. Her novels have been variously named to annual best books lists of the American Library Association, *Kirkus Reviews*, *Publishers Weekly*, *School Library Journal*, the *Guardian*, the New York Public Library, and the Los Angeles Public Library, and have been translated into many languages. She lives in Salt Lake City with her husband and online at SaraZarr.com.